Ride the Darkness

By

Craig Michael

DISCLAIMER:

Prologue

The Gulf Coast was a postcard at dusk, emerald waves, sugar-white sand, and a sky bleeding orange into the sea. But paradise had a shadow, and tonight it stretched long across Tampa's cracked sidewalks.

Alena Hernandez pressed her toes into the warm sand, trying to memorize the feeling, the illusion of safety. Nineteen, broke, and far from home, she'd learned the city's rhythms: keep your head down, move quick, trust no one. But desperation had a way of making you ignore instincts. That's how she ended up at the pirate bar, the one with the plastic skulls and checkered floors, sitting across from Sofia, a woman whose smile was too smooth to be real.

The drink was sweet, but it burned like gasoline. The world spun, shadows stretched, and the last thing Alena saw before darkness swallowed her was Sofia's hand, steady and cold, sliding her phone off the table.

She woke in the back of a moving car, wrists zip-tied, strangers' faces leering down. "Where am I?" she croaked, panic clawing at her throat.

"Nowhere you want to be, sweetheart," a man in the front seat sneered.

Two weeks vanished. Alena's parents haunted the police with desperate calls, her face became another missing poster on a bulletin board, until the file landed on the desk of Detective Nicole Beemer. Rookie, relentless, haunted by her own sister's disappearance years before. She saw something in Alena's eyes, a flicker of defiance, a shadow of fear, that dragged old wounds to the surface.

Nicole stared at the photo. "Where are you, Alena?" she whispered to the empty office. She'd break every rule, risk her badge and her life, to bring one girl back from the darkness.

But in the city's underbelly, evil wore a politician's smile and a badge. The Ring's reach stretched from the docks to city hall, and every minute Alena was missing, the shadows grew bolder.

Tonight, the hunt began.

ACKNOWLEDGMENTS

I would like to express my sincere gratitude to my wife for inspiring to write this book. She has been listening to my ideas for years and finally encouraged me to write them down. If it weren't for her, this book would never have happened. I truly enjoyed this process immensely.

I want to thank Charlotte Betrice, Cher Williger and Deana Markel for their early reading, opinions, reviews and suggestions of my first couple of drafts, they were invaluable.

To the boys, the real boys. These are my friends who inspired many of the characters in the book. I would go to the deepest depths for you all.

To the other individuals who inspired several of the main characters in this novel (you know who you are). My last lesson as a training officer would be, you never know how you are going to affect someone, so always do your best.

Dedication

I want to dedicate this book to my son *Colton*, you never really got to live your life and the life that you did live was full of pain. Until I see you again…

"Greater love has no one than this, to lay down one's life for his friends."

-John 15:13

CHAPTER 1: HOW IT BEGINS

The Gulf Coast unfurled like a watercolor dreamscape: emerald waves lapped at endless stretches of sugar-white sand so fine it squeaked underfoot, while palm trees swayed in the balmy, salt-tinged air. Tourists strolled lazily, toes sinking into powdery quartz, their laughter drifting on the breeze like music from another world. Here, sunsets bled pink and orange across a tranquil sea, and the warmth of the climate and spirit drew vacationers from every corner, eager to bask in barefoot luxury and the easy rhythm of paradise, if only for a moment.

But paradise wears a mask, and masks sometimes slip, occasionally all at once.

Alena Hernandez pressed her toes into the sand, trying to memorize the feeling, the illusion of safety woven into the heat on her skin and the salt on her tongue. At nineteen, a USF freshman scraping by in Tampa, Florida, she was far from Madison, Indiana, where the world always felt too small and her dreams too big to breathe. Now, she juggled classes she could barely afford, hunted for work with more desperation than hope, and tried not to look lost in a city that devoured the naïve and spat them out beneath flickering streetlights.

The bus stop on Nebraska Avenue was her last stop before home, until the day everything changed, and nothing familiar felt safe again. That afternoon, when the sun was burning low, quietly painting the city in gold, the light stretched across the sidewalks and street signs. Alena waited, her headphones in, eyes casually scanning the street with quiet vigilance, she tried not to zone out too deeply. She didn't even notice the woman until she sat beside her, a polished lady in her thirties, with sharp eyes and an easy smile with perfume that cut through the bus fumes like an unplaceable memory.

"You look like you've had a long day," the woman said, her voice warm, practiced, almost too smooth to be spontaneous.

Alena hesitated, startled by the kindness and wary of its intent. "Oh, yeah. I've got my classes, and I'm looking for a job. You know, just got a lot on my plate right now."

The woman grinned, flashing perfect teeth that didn't quite reach her eyes. "Oh, I know, I know. I've been there, girl." She extended a well-manicured, hand. "I'm Sofia. And if you don't mind me saying, you look like you could use a break."

Alena smiled, accepting Sofia's handshake. "Alena." Releasing Sofia's hand, she fiddled with items in her backpack, her keys, a notebook, a half-crumpled flyer, anything to ground herself. Then she spoke again, her voice tentative. "Sofia, if I'm honest, what I could really use is a job."

Sofia leaned back, appraising, then forward, lowering her voice as if sharing a secret. "Well, Alena, this might just be your lucky day," she said, with her smile wide, using that practiced charm flickering again.

Alena paused mid-motion, eyes narrowing with a flicker of hope. "Oh, yeah? How's that?"

"I happen to own a small café downtown, nothing big, mind you, and I need some help." Sofia looked at Alena with something akin to motherly affection, her head tilted just so. "I think you'd be perfect."

Alena's heart skipped, the weight of constant rejection lifting for a moment. "Seriously? I mean… yeah, I really am."

Sofia's gaze lingered a little too long, a little too intent, like a predator sizing up prey. "Meet me here tomorrow." She scribbled an address on a napkin and handed it to Alena with manicured fingers. "It's right around the corner from the café. We can talk details over drinks. My treat."

Alena hesitated, a prickle of unease brushing the back of her neck. But Sofia's warmth disarmed her, and the promise of a fresh start, the thing she'd chased for months, drowned out her doubts. "Okay. Great."

The next evening, Alena found herself in a dimly lit bar with nicotine-stained walls, checkered tile flooring, and graffiti-laced corridors twisting behind her. The interior was intimate, adorned with nautical artifacts, overhead fish nets, and carved woodwork evoking the belly of a pirate ship. The air was thick with cigarette smoke and the scent of spilled beer, a cocktail of grime and nostalgia. Sofia waved her over, already perched at a corner table as if she owned the place.

"You made it!" Sofia met her halfway, enveloping her in a hug as if they'd known each other for years.

"This is quite the place," Alena said, glancing around hesitantly.

"Oh, yeah, it's one of those pirate bars big around here. It's close to the café and part of the historic district. The bar opened in 1949."

They sat, and Sofia slid a drink across the table. "To new beginnings."

Alena eyed the glass, red, fizzy, too festive for the setting. "What's in it?"

"Just a little something to take the edge off. You trust me, right?"

The drink tasted sweet like candy on the front end but burned like gasoline on the back end. Not too bad, Alena thought. The two made small talk for what seemed like an hour. But then, time seemed to slow down. Alena wasn't sure how long she had been there at all. The room began to spin, slowly at first, then violently.

Alena forced a smile, her stomach tightening; a warning bell rang in the back of her mind. She took another sip. Sofia's smile twisted, her features blurring at the edges. The bar's shadows stretched and coiled, alive with secrets and whispers Alena couldn't quite hear.

The pirate décor, plastic skulls, faded flags, a rusty cutlass nailed to the wall, shimmered, their edges glowing with a soft, impossible light, as if part of a dream she'd entered and couldn't escape.

Panic began to crash over her. The walls leaned in, breathing, the wood grain swirling into faces, some grinning, others leering, all watching. Alena squeezed her eyes shut, but the visions intensified: she saw swirling galaxies behind her eyelids, a kaleidoscope of color and sound, memories and fears blending into an endless loop. Then everything faded to black.

When she woke, an engine's hum buzzed in her head, low and steady, like a warning she couldn't shake. Leather seats clung to her bare arms, sticky with sweat and fear. She was in the backseat of a moving car, with strangers' faces leering down upon her, blurred, unfamiliar, very wrong. A man's laugh oozed out, slow and sickeningly sweet. Everything was wrong.

She tried to move but couldn't. Her wrists were zip-tied, tight. Her phone and ID were gone. Panic began to claw at her throat, desperate to escape.

"Where am I?" she croaked, her voice raw and cracking.

A man in the front seat laughed. "Nowhere you want to be, sweetheart."

She twisted hard, wrists burning against the zip ties. "Let me out! Please!"

"Just shut up," a woman snapped, shoving her back with excessive force. The city outside the window was blurred, indifferent and endless, neon and asphalt smeared across the glass like a dream she was already forgetting.

Two weeks vanished.

Alena's parents, frantic, haunted the local police with desperate calls and sleepless nights. Her mother's voice cracked with each plea: "She's not the type to run away. Please, you have to find her." Her father's fists were white on the steering wheel, scouring the city for any sign, as if he could just will her back by sheer force of love.

Their daughter was so eager for her new life, but now she had become another missing face on a bulletin board, another silent file buried in a detective's inbox.

But this file happened to land on the desk of Detective Nicole Beemer, a rookie with a reputation for stubbornness bordering on obsession. She wasn't just an eager investigator chasing a name for herself; she saw a girl with a family, a future stolen from her, and she couldn't let it go. Photos of missing kids blurred past, but Alena's face stopped her cold.

Something in those eyes, a flicker of defiance, a shadow of fear, it clawed at Nicole's own scars. Fifteen years ago, her own sister had vanished. There were no leads and no closure. The local cops had ticked every box, closed every file, but Nicole knew the truth: sometimes, the world swallows you whole and doesn't spit you back out.

Beemer rarely spoke of her sister, but the wound shaped her. They were carved into her bones, fueling her relentless drive to find the missing, to drag the truth into the light, no matter how ugly. She stared at Alena's file, her jaw tight. This wasn't just a case, it was a reckoning.

She was ready to tear the city apart to find what others had missed. In Alena Hernandez, she saw a daughter, a granddaughter, a sister. Her mentor's voice echoed: "Treat every victim like she's your own."

She stared at Alena's photo, determined. Her whisper broke the stillness of the empty office: "Where are you, Alena?"

Her partner, Detective Todd Greene, leaned over her shoulder. "Another runaway, Nicole? Or you think there's more?"

Nicole's eyes flashed, sharp and certain. "She didn't run. Look at the timeline. Look at her last text to her mom, she was scared. Someone took her."

Greene sighed, rubbing his neck, weariness etched into his movements. "Most runaways come back, you know. You're banking on the worst case, Nicole."

Nicole's hand curled into a fist, the file crinkling beneath her fingers. "No. This one was taken. We've got to find her. Whatever it takes."

Greene hesitated. "You know what the chief said about those, right? Gotta have approval from the lieutenant to work them. Do you... have approval on this one?"

"Yeah, yeah, I know what he said," Beemer snapped. She raised her voice, "The LT isn't looking at these cases! You don't think there's a small chance I see something he doesn't?" Her tone was sharp, filled with frustration.

Greene waved her off. "Alright, do what you want. It's your career."

She glared at him. "I've got to do something, Todd. I can't just sit here, day after day, watching these cases cross my desk and do nothing! Why do they get to pick which girls matter, huh? You ever think about that?"

"I don't know," Greene shrugged. "Maybe they're just trying to prioritize. Focus on the ones with the highest probability of success, you know?"

"So what's the job title then?" Beemer shot back. "Homicide and Missing Persons? Or just Homicide and easy cases now?"

"Hey, I'm just saying what the chief and LT said. Take it for what it's worth," Greene muttered, already backing away.

She ignored him, dialing Alena's number again, knowing it would ring into silence. The ringtone buzzed in her ear like a countdown. The clock was ticking, and the city's underbelly was about to bleed secrets.

Nicole Beemer was ready to break the rules, risking her badge, her reputation, maybe even her life, to bring one girl back from the darkness.

And somewhere, in the shadows of paradise, Alena was waiting, hoping someone would come.

CHAPTER 2: THE HOOK

Beemer's scarf scraped her skin like sandpaper as she stepped into Tampa's port, a graveyard of rusted shipping containers and diesel fumes. The air reeked of saltwater and fuel as the faint cries of gulls screamed overhead. Here, she was no longer Detective Nicole Beemer, she was just another nameless face in a sea of desperation.

Weeks of undercover work had led her inside The Ring, a ruthless human trafficking syndicate thriving in the shadows, smuggling human cargo through the waterways.

Tonight's mission was simple: observe, gather intel, and stay invisible. Find Alena.

But simplicity unraveled fast.

It had been months since she'd spoken with Amanda Collins, an independent YouTube investigator. Beemer had stumbled across her channel, November Collins, while chasing leads in the internet's dark corners, videos exposing political corruption in Tampa Bay and possible ties to human trafficking.

Beemer's mind drifted to her field training, every lesson drilled into her by Colt, her old training officer. He was relentless and tough as nails, but never unfair. Colt was a walking armory, each lesson a live round. "Always watch the hands," he'd bark. "Trust your backup."

Tonight, there was no backup. No cavalry. Just Beemer, alone in the dark, with Colt's voice echoing in her head. He'd hate this. He'd call her reckless. And he'd be right.

She'd left that department years after training, chasing bigger cases, bigger risks. Undercover work had called to her like a siren song, an itch she couldn't ignore. Colt had warned her: "Your time will come. Patience." But he never chained her down. He knew she was built for more.

Now, deep in enemy territory, she hunted the core of a human trafficking syndicate with tentacles reaching into city hall and the police force itself. Corruption oozed through every layer, greasing palms, erasing evidence, buying silence. The knowledge made her skin crawl.

Why did the chief and lieutenant pick and choose which cases to investigate? It hadn't made sense until she spotted a pattern, it was subtle, almost undetectable, but there. If she was right, the ramifications were massive.

How did they sleep at night? How did they face themselves while innocents vanished into the shadows? There was no one left to trust. Not tonight. Not in this city. If she fell, no one would come. But if she succeeded, she'd burn their empire to the ground.

This was bigger than her. Lives hung in the balance, real people, real danger. Alena Hernandez had been spotted in the area just a week ago. A college friend had tried to reach her, but before he could get close, she was dragged off by men who didn't care who saw. Beemer had spent hours on the phone with Alena's parents, John and Carmen. They weren't just voices anymore; they felt like family.

"Don't get emotionally involved," Colt used to say.

I know, I know, Beemer thought, but how could she not? She spent weeks chasing shadows, piecing together scraps. It had brought her to the edge. There was no turning back now. She plunged in, headfirst, heart pounding, ready to face whatever waited in the dark.

A sharp whistle sliced through the humid night, followed by hurried footsteps. She froze, pulse hammering, as she spotted two burly men dragging a young woman toward a rusted cargo container. The girl's muffled screams clawed at the silence, her hands scraping the ground in futile resistance. Every instinct urged her to act, but she couldn't blow her cover, not yet. Instead, she slipped closer, boots whispering against the damp pavement.

"Move it!" one man snarled, shoving the girl into the container and slamming the door with a deafening clang.

Beemer's heart thundered as their eyes swept the yard, and landed on her. The weight of that glance felt like ice sliding down her spine.

"You!" The taller man jabbed a finger in her direction, his gaze sharp and suspicious. "What are you doing out here?"

Beemer forced a tremble into her voice, lowering her gaze and clutching her scarf like armor. "I, I got lost," she stammered, making herself smaller.

Her fingers tightened around the fabric, willing herself to stay in character, a frightened girl in the wrong place. She didn't dare meet his eyes.

The shorter man sneered, stepping closer, his presence suffocating. "Lost? You look like you belong in there with the others."

His breath reeked of tobacco and cruelty, the kind of man

who thrived on fear. Beemer held her ground, though her knees begged to buckle. Her stomach churned as he grabbed her arm and yanked her forward. She stumbled but didn't resist, defiance would raise alarms she couldn't afford. Her mind raced: no backup, no contingency plan. If they discovered her identity, she'd be dead before dawn.

"Check her," the taller man barked.

Rough hands pawed at her coat and jeans, searching for anything incriminating. Her badge was safely hidden in her car, the one precaution she hadn't compromised, but a flicker of hesitation could betray her. She stayed loose, pliable, like she had nothing to hide. Biting the inside of her cheek anchored her. One wrong breath, one wrong twitch, and everything would unravel.

As the shorter man stepped closer, Beemer's mind spiraled into survival mode. Training blurred with instinct, a vivid sequence playing out like a movie, fast and unforgiving. She imagined seizing his hand, clamping down on his palm, twisting his wrist against its natural angle, and yanking downward. A guttural groan would escape him, choked by surprise. Momentum would surge through her like a fuse catching flame.

She'd pivot sharply toward the taller man, her boot lashing out in a brutal side kick to his knee. It would buckle with a sickening crack, and he'd crumple like dead weight. Colt's voice echoed: "The bigger they are, the harder they fall, and a good kick to the balls is always fair game." She almost smiled. Almost.

Then she'd focus on the shorter man. With his arm secured, she'd wrap her leg around it, locking it in place, and deliver a donkey kick to shatter his elbow with a loud crunch. The movement would be flawless, instinctive, brutal, the joint giving way beneath the force.

But then,

Reality snapped her back like ice water. "No!" she thought. She couldn't. Not yet. She needed to stay under the radar, to play this smart. Answers first, then justice. Her breath hitched, heart pounding from the ghost of an action she hadn't taken. The threat remained, but so did her mission. Timing was everything.

Whoever was behind The Ring would pay. But first, she had to save the girls who couldn't save themselves.

"She's clean... real clean," the shorter man drawled, his smile stretching too wide, eyes glinting with something feral. The silence hung heavy, suffocating, before he broke it. "What do you say we take this one for a little test drive?"

His partner's lips twisted into a smirk that knotted Beemer's stomach. "Sounds like fun, but Mr. Morales wouldn't like that," he said, voice oily and low, fingers flicking in mocking air quotes. "You know he likes them 'undriven.'"

The air felt colder. Beemer didn't flinch, didn't breathe, just watched, calculating. Rage swirled beneath her skin, but she kept her face blank. Not yet. Timing was everything. The girls were counting on her.

The shorter man's grin widened, flashing a jagged gold grill. "But Mr. Morales ain't here, is he? And I feel like going for a loooong drive tonight."

Every muscle in Beemer's body coiled, adrenaline burning, screaming to fight, to run, to do anything but wait.

"Let's just get her inside," the partner snapped, impatience sharpening his tone.

The men closed in, shadows stretching in the dim light. Beemer braced herself, fingers twitching instinctively toward her boot, where her knife would have been. But it wasn't there, not tonight. She hesitated, a fraction too long. The taller man shoved her against the container door, his breath hot against her ear as he growled: "Don't make me angry, darlin'. Or I will be taking that drive after all!"

Shuddering, Beemer swallowed hard, forcing down the panic clawing her throat. She nodded stiffly, feigning submission, and stepped into the suffocating darkness of the shipping container.

The metallic clang of the door slamming shut echoed like a gunshot, a death sentence reverberating through steel walls. The lock snapped into place with chilling finality.

Inside, the air reeked of sweat and urine. A girl beside her trembled, whispering prayers that melted into the distant rattle of chains. Half a dozen women huddled on the freezing steel floor, their faces pale and hollow. Wide, terrified eyes flicked to Beemer, searching for answers, or hope.

She fought to steady her breathing as she lowered herself beside them, resisting the urge to recoil from the raw terror radiating from their shivering bodies.

A young woman with tangled hair and a split lip whispered, "Did they hurt you? Did they say what they want?" Her voice quivered, barely rising above the frantic breathing and muffled sobs.

Beemer shook her head, forcing her voice to sound as shattered as the others'. "No… just shoved me in here. I, I don't know what's happening." She let her voice crack, hoping to blend in, to disappear.

"They took my sister last week," another woman choked out, clutching her knees to her chest. "Said she was 'ready for market.' I haven't seen her since."

A third woman, older, her voice brittle with exhaustion, muttered, "Don't talk too much. They listen sometimes. You never know who's working for them."

Beemer's mind raced, adrenaline surging, every sense on high alert. No weapons. No backup. No way out, yet. But she had one advantage: they didn't know who she was. If she could hold her cover long enough, she might gather intel, find a weakness, an opening, anything to turn this nightmare into leverage against The Ring.

She glanced at her pocket, feeling the slim outline of her emergency burner phone tucked beneath her waistband. One text to Tally, and this op would go hot. Just a name. A number scrawled on a scrap of paper. A desperate, last-ditch gamble she'd hoped never to use.

But was it worth burning her cover?

If things went sideways, it might be her only lifeline.

A sudden bang on the container wall made everyone flinch. "Quiet in there!" a voice barked from outside, muffled but menacing.

The women shrank back, their hope flickering out like a candle in the wind. Beemer leaned in, whispering to the woman beside her, "Stay calm. Watch and listen. We'll get out of this. I promise."

The words were as much for herself as for them.

For now, Nicole Beemer wasn't a detective. She wasn't even Nicole. She was just another victim, trapped in the dark belly of despair, fighting to survive, and waiting for her moment to strike.

CHAPTER 3: RETIREMENT.... KINDA

The day had finally come: retirement. Twenty-five years of service, wrapped in blood, sweat, and the kind of memories that like to surface when the world gets too quiet. Colt would get his little send-off: the ceremonial handshake from the chief, polite applause from a room full of uniforms, and the official passing of the badge. The department also let him keep his gun.

The shiny, newly issued Sig Sauer P320 RXP 9mm. Colt scowled. He would have preferred to keep his old P320 with the iron sights. That gun was a perfect extension of his hand. He knew every groove, every weight shift, every quirk. It had history. This new one? It was strange, cold, precise, soulless.

Retirement meant no more long shifts. No more death calls. No more domestics with shattered coffee tables and blood on the walls. No more late-night phone calls that jerked him out of bed and straight into someone else's tragedy. No more rookies like Beemer, wide-eyed, overeager, and always two steps behind reality.

Colt had plans for retirement, plans to do a whole lot of nothing. Just peace, stillness, and maybe a porch swing if he could find one that didn't creak. He and Becca had talked about traveling for years, tossing around ideas like breadcrumbs on a map, especially that trip to Scotland. Now it was finally within reach, the kind of dream you didn't have to fold up and shelve anymore.

But after decades on the road, Colt wasn't the same man he used to be. The job had carved lines into him deeper than time ever could. He still woke to the same nightmare, Sergeant Patton's voice, cut off mid-laugh, the Humvee explosion seared behind his eyelids like a brand. He'd come awake in a cold sweat, fists clenched, heart pounding like war drums.

Becca stirred beside him, already knowing. "Again?" she whispered, voice thick with sleep and worry. He didn't answer. He couldn't. Some things didn't need words.

No amount of wellness training or mental health seminars could undo that kind of wear and tear. He tried, though, for Becca's sake, for the woman who stayed, who steadied him.

Politics had kept him from climbing the ranks, from playing the game others seemed to thrive in. But he'd never wanted a desk job anyway. Special positions or Investigations upstairs never held any real appeal. That wasn't him. That was never him.

Coming from a military family, Colt had always identified as a soldier first. The son of two career military parents, his childhood had been a blur of base housing, flag ceremonies, and the low rumble of moving trucks and helicopters overhead every couple of years. Discipline, duty, and displacement were part of the air he breathed. So, it felt natural, even inevitable, to try out for SWAT. Not just for the thrill, not just for the brotherhood, but for the rigorous order that came with it. For the sense that chaos could be contained if you were trained enough to meet it head-on.

The training offered a chance to sharpen his skills further. Colt's career wasn't chosen, it was shouldered, like a ruck sack that he'd never set down. Heavy from the start. He didn't walk into the job so much as inherit the weight of it, carrying it forward like a legacy carved into his bones.

Physically, Colt had held up well, until the last few years began carving their own stories into his body. The job had taken its toll: four surgeries in three years, a neck fusion, two knee operations, and a shoulder repair. Titanium, scar tissue, and willpower held him together more than muscle now.

By the end of his career, he felt like he was falling apart. Each movement came with a reminder. Each day, a negotiation with pain. Deep down, he knew the guys on the team were cutting him slack because of his tenure, because of the years he'd bled for the job, for them. Hell, he'd trained most of them anyway, brought them up from green to gritty.

No one stayed on SWAT as long as Colt. Not because they couldn't, but because they wouldn't. The wear, the weight, the risk, it burned most out by year ten. But Colt had kept going, as if quitting meant giving up something sacred.

His reign as team leader ended a few years ago, after a car accident sidelined him for months. A T-bone at an intersection, nothing dramatic, nothing heroic. Just bad timing and a distracted driver. When he returned, everything had shifted. The team had adapted without him, and though no one said it out loud, he could feel it. He wasn't sure where he fit in anymore.

Then a sniper position opened up, a coveted spot, the kind that didn't come around often, and Colt decided to go for it. The assessment was brutal, designed to weed out anyone who couldn't handle the mental grind or physical demand. But Colt trained relentlessly, obsessed over every shot, every movement, every breath. And he surprised everyone, maybe even himself, by acing it.

That's when he truly earned the "OG" title. Not just out of respect for his years, but because he'd proved he still had it. Still dangerous. Still disciplined.

Sniping suited him. It was about precision. Quiet control. The ability to sit still and wait. It was solitary, no need for small talk or second opinions. Just decisions made in silence, and the sharp, controlled exhale that followed a perfect shot. And most importantly, it was shooting, pure, stripped-down skill.

Colton Alexander Flynn was fifty-five years old, retiring with twenty-five years of service as a law enforcement officer. He had the plaques, the commendations, the scars.

Yet, being a police officer was never his dream.

Colt enlisted in the Army right out of high school, young, restless, and looking for a fight. He went Infantry, for some reason. Later, with the hindsight only years and surgeries could provide, he'd think, I should've gone in the Air Force, the food is better.

Colt served honorably in Desert Storm, earned his stripes the hard way, and was awarded a Bronze Star. Not that he ever talked about it much.

After the Army, Colt pursued college, surprising even himself. He earned a degree in World History, a field as far removed from law enforcement as one could imagine. No guns. No protocols. Just dusty civilizations and the stories they left behind.

It was during this time he met Becca, smart, steady, kind in a way that disarmed him completely. He fell deeply in love, and for the first time, started thinking about building something instead of surviving everything. They got married. Started a family. Life seemed set on a quiet course, a gentle slope into something normal.

Colt's career trajectory would have been locked in, maybe teaching, maybe research, if it hadn't been for 9/11. A day that split time, rewrote priorities, and changed everything. The towers fell, and so did the illusion that his fight was done.

Colt re-enlisted in the Guard, a familiar weight settling back on his shoulders like an old rucksack. He began Officer Candidate School (OCS), driven by a sense of duty, of unfinished business. He wasn't chasing glory, just doing what he was made to do.

Colt received his military commission, was assigned to the infantry as a Platoon Leader, and deployed to Afghanistan. He always believed there was no greater honor than leading men into battle. To have them trust and follow you with their lives, that was a privilege beyond measure. His unit saw more action than most reservist outfits, but Colt always viewed it simply as part of his duty.

He came close to taking an insurgent's bullet just outside of Marjah, if it hadn't been for his Platoon Sergeant, Lloyd Patton. "Watch out there, sir. Can't be losing one of the few good officers we have," Patton had said.

Colt was always proud of his service, but humble, too. Enlisted men respected officers who had risen through their ranks. "Mustangs," they called them. An officer who had once been enlisted knew what it was like to clean toilets, get assigned KP duty, and stand late-night guard.

Sergeant Patton was later killed by an IED when his Humvee struck it during a simple convoy mission delivering supplies to the FOB. Colt took it particularly hard, the old, crusty vet had reminded him of his father. It was a loss that stung deep, because Patton was one of the few men who truly understood what it meant to lead from the front.

Two years later, Colt's son was only six months old when he received orders for his second tour. Becca was beside herself. They had been dealing with Colt Jr.'s rare heart condition since well before he was born, diagnosed at 22 weeks. It had been an extremely stressful year for both of them, especially for Becca, who did her best to make life feel normal for their daughter, five-year-old Aislyn.

When Colt Jr. passed away, Colt knew he just couldn't leave Becca again, especially after that. He resigned his commission. Family comes first.

Police work suited Colt in ways he hadn't anticipated. He'd always been good with people, talking to them, understanding them, and his age gave him an edge over younger recruits. Not to mention his vast and eclectic work history. He brought maturity and life experience to the job, qualities that proved invaluable in navigating the complexities of right and wrong, especially when so much of the job existed in the inevitable shades of gray.

Early on, Colt discovered that a cop's best weapon was his mouth. Persuasion could defuse situations far more effectively than force. But he also learned, sometimes the hard way, that words could escalate conflict just as quickly.

Colt did pretty much everything, instructorships, legal classes, seminars, case studies, you name it. He became an instructor for Firearms, Defensive Tactics, Active Assailants, SWAT Tactics, and Sniper, all while training recruits on the basics of being a cop.

It was several years in as an FTO, or Field Training Officer, when Recruit Nicole "Nikki" Beemer stepped into his cruiser. Colt immediately liked her, something he usually would never admit. She was fresh out of the Army and smart as a whip. Colt always enjoyed training veterans; there was usually an instant rapport. He also knew he could typically count on a certain level of discipline from someone who had served.

She reminded him of his own daughter, strong, determined, and fiercely intelligent. Nicole, or "Beemer" as Colt called her, ended up extended with him past the recommended four weeks of field training due to a bad hurricane season. Six weeks in a car together was a long time, but the two of them had a blast, swapping war stories and telling jokes only military people would understand.

Becca would joke that Beemer was one of the few recruits Colt never said he wanted to choke out. He always said she was way too smart for the department. Too smart to be a cop.

Few officers could handle being an FTO for more than a few years. Colt did it for well over fifteen. He would've kept doing it, too, until some genius lieutenant decided he couldn't be a SWAT operator, SWAT sniper, instructor, and FTO all at the same time. They told him he had to make a choice.

By that time, after years of dealing with recruits and the slimy politics that came with it, the decision was easy. He turned in the trainer pin and never looked back.

But now, as retirement loomed, Colt couldn't shake the feeling that it wasn't just his body that was falling apart, it was his mind. He had a lot of time on his hands now. Too much time.

Colt stared at the cellphone on the table, its screen dark and silent. No more late-night phone calls, he promised himself. No more ghosts from the past clawing their way into the present.

But as the words faded in his mind, the phone lit up, its harsh ringtone slicing through the silence like a warning shot. The number was blocked. Colt's jaw tightened. He could almost feel the chill of old ghosts gathering in the corners of the room, waiting to see if he'd answer.

CHAPTER 4: THE RING

Just beyond the festive lights and food trucks of Sparkman's Wharf, past the roars and cheers of Amalie Arena on the outskirts of Tampa's bustling port, the air was heavy with saltwater and secrets, thick enough to taste. The distant moan of cargo ships reverberated through the cavernous warehouse, a low, ominous drone that mingled with the faint clang of rigging and the occasional shriek of a gull echoing off metal and concrete. Crates with stamped foreign insignia loomed overhead, stacked into towers that carved a labyrinth of shadows, each one darker than the last. The only illumination came from a single overhead bulb, its glow flickering and sputtering with stubborn resistance, casting long silhouettes that danced across the floor like ghosts with nowhere left to haunt.

At the center of this makeshift fortress stood Jan Morales, a man whose reputation slithered through the city's underbelly. His name wasn't whispered, it hissed. Dressed in a jet-black leather suit that gleamed even in the dim light, Morales exuded a predatory confidence. He didn't just walk into a room, he owned its air. His eyes were sharp and cold, they swept across the room as he addressed the group of men gathered around a battered table. Maps of shipping routes and ledgers filled with cryptic numbers and coded transactions lay strewn before them, the paper edges curling with humidity. The room smelled of rust, sweat, and secrets.

Morales's voice sliced through the tension, smooth as silk but edged with steel. "We can't be having these loose ends, boys." He paused, letting the words hang. Heavy. Measured. Dangerous. "You all remember what happened to the last guy who got sloppy, don't you?"

A nervous shuffle rippled through the group. One man, sweat beading on his brow, glanced toward the far corner where a sealed fifty-five-gallon drum sat atop a bloodstained tarp. No one spoke. No one had to. The implication was clear, and no one dared speak.

Morales's enforcers, two hulking men in dark jackets, their faces obscured by the brims of their caps, stood stoically behind him. Their presence was a silent warning, their silence more threatening than any words. Like statues carved from violence, they didn't blink, didn't breathe too loudly. They didn't need to.

From the shadows, Deputy Chief Randall Hayes of the Tampa Port Authority and Airport Police leaned against a crate, the gold badge on his chest catching the light with every shift. He lit a cigarette, the flare briefly illuminating his weathered face, and exhaled a plume of smoke that curled lazily toward the rafters. He looked like a man who'd made peace with his compromises or at least learned to smoke through them.

"You've got my guys keeping the streets real quiet. But the real threat is not the strays, it's the wolves. They don't miss," Hayes said, his voice gravelly and low. "No one's getting near this place unless I say so. Not even a stray dog." He took another drag, the ember glowing like the fuse of something buried and ticking.

Morales grinned, his white teeth flashed. "That's why we keep you around, Chief. Loyalty like yours is a rare commodity these days. Isn't that right, boys?"

One of the men at the table, a wiry guy with a nervous twitch, tried to muster a laugh, but it came out as a strangled cough. Another muttered, "Yeah, right," barely audible. Another snickered. The table creaked under the weight of unspoken fear.

Hayes flicked ash onto the floor, his gaze sweeping over the group. "Just remember who's sticking his neck out here. If this goes sideways-"

Morales cut him off, his voice dropping to a near whisper. "If this goes sideways, Chief, you'll be washing up in the bay, if there's anything left to find, that is." The words floated out like smoke, soft, slow and lethal. A tense silence settled over the room, broken only by the distant clang of metal and the relentless thrum of the port outside, like the heartbeat of a beast that never slept.

In the shadowed corner, a nameless young woman chained to a chair stirred. Her face was bruised, one eye swollen nearly shut, but her gaze burned with a fierce, unbroken defiance. Blood had dried at the corner of her mouth, but she didn't flinch. She shifted, the shackles clinking like wind chimes in a storm, and drew the attention of the entire room.

Morales strode over, his footsteps echoing like gunshots on concrete. He crouched to her level, his face inches from hers, the stench of stale tobacco and sweat hanging between them. "You think someone's coming for you?" he sneered, voice low and mocking. "This port is ours. The cops?" He waved his hand toward Chief Hayes, lounging in the back with his badge half-tucked and his conscience long gone. "Bought and paid for. We control more than you can even dream."

The woman, Maya Cruz, glared at him, her face clenched so tightly it trembled. Not that they knew her name, at least, not yet. Maya had been taken two weeks prior while on vacation with her fiancé, during what should have been the first days of their honeymoon. She had continued to be defiant, a wildfire refusing to be snuffed out.

Glaring at Morales, her voice cut through the heavy air with a thick Latin accent. "You're wrong," she spat, voice hoarse but steady. "Someone's coming. And when they do, you'll wish you'd never, "

Before she could finish, one of Morales's enforcers stepped forward and struck her across the face. The crack echoed through the warehouse like a gunshot. She slumped sideways, blood trickling from her lip, but her eyes, those furious, unblinking eyes, never left Morales's.

Little did Maya know, her fiancé, the man whose hand she'd held on the beach in Brazil, who had sworn forever, had sold her to the slavers to pay off a spiralling gambling debt he'd hidden for months. He'd arranged the entire setup when they visited Tampa, luring her with soft smiles while orchestrating her betrayal.

Morales wiped his cheek with a crisp handkerchief, a dark chuckle rumbling from his chest like distant thunder. "You've got spirit," he said, standing.

"But spirit doesn't pay the bills. Or buy you freedom."

Hayes watched, his expression unreadable. "She's more trouble than she's worth, Morales," he muttered. "We don't need heat right now, not with the locals sniffing around." He looked down and adjusted a HENSLEY campaign pin on his uniform.

Morales shot him a look. "Relax, Chief. No one's sniffing anywhere they shouldn't, not with you on our payroll."

A sudden crash outside made everyone jump. The enforcers reached for their weapons, eyes darting toward the doors. The sound of waves crashing against the docks grew louder, like the bay itself was protesting the evil unfolding within these walls.

Morales raised a hand, signalling for steady. "Check it out, boys."

Several enforcers drew their weapons and stealthily walked outside.

Morales looked at Maya, smiling. "Probably just a stray cat. Or a nosy reporter who won't be nosy much longer."

But beneath his bravado, a flicker of doubt crossed his face. He glanced at Hayes, who met his gaze with a thin, humorless smile.

The Ring believed themselves untouchable, their power absolute, their secrets safe.

Morales's laughter echoed through the warehouse, mingling with the restless night. For now, The Ring operated untouchable. But somewhere in the city, the true leader watched from behind a politician's mask, confident that his double life remained hidden.

For now.

But evil like this doesn't survive alone, it needs protectors. It must be contained rather than eliminated. There must be balance. The balance between evil and good is a shifting, contested space where every choice carries consequences, and no one escapes unscathed.

CHAPTER 5: LIVING THE QUIET LIFE

Colt sat on his back porch, the faded wood creaking beneath him as he leaned back, letting the salty morning breeze roll in from the bay. The bay stretched out, calm like a graveyard. Colt hated graveyards. The air carried the sharp tang of seaweed, mingling with the citrusy scent of his Tequila Sunrise. He took a slow sip, savoring the burn. Sure, it was only 9 a.m., but he'd kicked the stigma of morning drinking to the curb years ago, midnight shifts had a way of erasing social conventions.

Colt slowly puffed on his Mayflower cigar, staring at the burnt end afterward as if to check if it was still lit. Another guilty pleasure of earned time. No one was judging him; besides, he was retired now. He'd earned the right to drink and smoke whenever the hell he pleased.

He was just about to close his eyes and let the sun warm his face when his phone vibrated against the weathered table. The shrill ring cut through the quiet, jarring him. Early calls were rare these days. Most people knew better than to bother him before noon. He eyed the phone, thumb hovering over the decline button. But something prickled at the back of his neck, a gut feeling he hadn't shaken since his days on the force.

With a sigh, he answered. "Flynn here," his voice rough as gravel.

There was a pause. Static crackled. Then, a thin, shaky voice: "Uh, hello? Is this Officer Flynn?"

Colt's lips curled into a wry smile. "Mr. Flynn," he corrected, barely shifting in his chair. "I'm retired. Don't call me 'Officer' unless you want me to hang up."

"Oh, right... um, sorry. I was told to call you if anything happened. I mean, if something went wrong."

Colt sat up straighter, old instincts kicking in. "If anything happened to who?" His tone sharpened, slicing through the morning calm. "What's this about?"

"Miss Nikki," the voice replied, hesitant, almost whispering the name.

Colt's pulse kicked like a shotgun racking. He squinted into the sunlight, his grip tightening around the sweating glass, tequila sloshing against his knuckles, burning like guilt.

"Beemer?" he asked, voice low and dangerous.

"Yeah, Nikki Beemer, the undercover cop," the caller clarified, words tumbling out too fast.

The last time he'd spoken with Beemer, it was about the corruption in her department. Should he have gotten more involved?

Colt's mind raced. He'd heard whispers from Bear about Beemer's latest assignment, something big, something ugly. She was deep undercover, working a human trafficking ring at the docks. The kind of operation that drew the worst kind of attention. She'd told him she planned to take it federal, blow the whole thing wide open. But if someone was calling him instead of the police…

He forced steel into his voice. "Who is this?" he demanded, every syllable clipped.

"Tally… I'm Tally. Nikki said to call you if something went wrong. She made me memorize your number. Said if I called anyone else… she'd disappear."

The voice cracked, panic bleeding through.

Colt stared out at the bay, its surface glassy and calm, mocking the storm brewing inside him.

"Why aren't you calling her team?" he pressed, suspicion sharpening his words.

"She can't trust them!" Tally's voice trembled, teetering on the edge of hysteria. "She said some of them were involved, dirty. Nikki said you were the only one she could rely on. She said if I called anyone else, I'd get her killed."

Colt's stomach twisted. He remembered Beemer's warnings about the rot spreading through the department, the way good men turned bad for a quick buck. He could almost hear her voice, fierce and afraid, telling him about the shadows closing in.

He took a long breath, fighting to keep his cool.

"And what exactly am I supposed to do? Walk in there with a shotgun and a retirement card?" he asked, voice like ice. "I'm not a cop anymore."

"There's no one else!" Tally's plea was raw, desperate. "Please, Mr. Flynn. If they find out she's a cop, they'll kill her. I think they already suspect something. Nikki said you'd know what to do. She trusted you."

Colt closed his eyes, the weight of old loyalty pressing down on him. Retirement had dulled his edge, but it hadn't erased his instincts or his sense of duty. He could almost feel the badge, heavy as a stone, pressing against his chest.

He opened his eyes, staring out at the horizon, where the sky met the restless sea.

"All right," he said finally, voice cold and steady as steel. "I'll see what I can do. But you need to stay put, Tally. Don't talk to anyone. Don't trust anyone. Not until I say so."

"O-okay. I won't. Please, hurry."

The line died like a flatline.

Colt stared at his phone, the silence ringing in his ears. He downed the rest of his drink in one burning gulp, the tequila igniting a fire in his gut.

Slowly, he rose from his chair, every muscle tense, every sense alert. His knees popped, old injuries protesting. The chair groaned as if it knew he wasn't coming back.

He gazed out over the bay, the peaceful morning shattered. Somewhere out there, Beemer was running out of time.

And Colt was all she had left.

CHAPTER 6: HIDDEN SNAKE

In the grand chamber of City Hall, the powerful and charismatic Mayor Victor Hensley presided over a meeting of civic leaders. The room hummed with the energy of progress, a current that seemed to pulse in sync with the city's ambition. Hensley, dressed in a tailored navy suit that sharpened his commanding silhouette, commanded attention with his booming voice and sharp intellect, a presence impossible to ignore.

Victor Hensley leaned forward at the mahogany conference table, his piercing gray eyes scanning the room like searchlights seeking signs of hesitation. The city's top officials sat before him, their faces a mix of admiration and deference, the unspoken weight of expectation heavy in the air.

"Ladies and gentlemen," he began, his voice steady and authoritative, cutting through the quiet with the precision of a practiced leader, "the redevelopment of the Port District is not just an economic initiative, it's a promise to our citizens. A promise that we will rebuild this city into a beacon of opportunity." He gestured to the architectural renderings projected on the screen behind him, the digital glow casting blue shadows across the polished table. "With this project, we'll create jobs, housing, and a future our children can be proud of." His words hung in the air, not as speculation, but as a declaration carved from conviction.

The applause was immediate and thunderous, echoing off the marble walls like a storm of approval. Hensley smiled, a politician's smile, practiced yet warm enough to disarm even his fiercest critics. The kind of smile that won elections and masked intentions. He nodded to his deputy, signalling the end of the public session with the smooth confidence of a man always in control.

As the officials filed out, their murmured conversations fading into the hallway, Hensley remained seated, tapping his fingers rhythmically on the table, each tap a metronome of calculated thought. When the last door closed, sealing him in solitude, he reached into his jacket pocket and retrieved a sleek black phone, the matte surface cool against his fingertips. A single swipe revealed an encrypted messaging app, its interface stark and silent.

He typed quickly: "Meeting tonight. Usual location. No delays."

The message pulsed once, then vanished into the ether.

Moments later, a reply flashed on the screen: "Understood." The word lingered like a whisper in the room, sterile and final.

Hensley stood and walked to the floor-to-ceiling windows overlooking the city skyline from atop City Hall, the lights of Tampa glittering through the rain-streaked glass like fractured stars. The city was quiet at this hour, but his mind was anything but, a tempest beneath the surface. He swirled a glass of bourbon, its amber glow catching on the heavy mahogany desk, an Ivy League graduation gift from parents who'd mistaken ambition for virtue, who believed achievement could substitute for understanding.

He never wanted any of this. Politics had always been their dream, not his. They'd sent him north to the finest colleges, hoping to polish away the rough edges, to make him a leader sculpted from prestige. They never saw what he really was, a boy who felt nothing, who watched other children cry and wondered why he couldn't, as if sorrow were a foreign dialect he was never taught. He remembered the small animals behind his childhood home, the way their fear had thrilled him, the power he felt as their world narrowed to just him and their pain. It was the only time he'd ever felt alive.

Now, as mayor, he commanded a city, and in the shadows, The Ring. His parents thought they'd given Tampa a savior. In truth, they'd handed it to a predator who'd only grown more cunning with age, shedding innocence like a skin he never needed. The city was his playground, its people pieces on a board he could move, break, or discard at will, each one unaware they were actors in a game scripted by his will.

Victor smiled, the expression never reaching his eyes. He raised his glass in a silent toast to the city below, to the empire he'd built in daylight and darkness alike, a kingdom carved from compromise and corruption. The Ring's next move was coming, and he relished the thought, not of power, but of control, of fear, of pain. Just as he always had. Control was his true addiction, more potent than wealth or applause.

Hensley stood, staring at the skyline. The Port District redevelopment was more than just a civic project, it was a carefully constructed façade, built on blueprints soaked in secrecy. Beneath its legitimate veneer lay his true ambition: expanding the operations of his organization, a sprawling human trafficking network that funnelled untold millions into his offshore accounts and claimed lives like shadows swallowing light. The city would never see it coming, because predators like him didn't hide in the dark. They thrived in plain sight.

Later in the evening, Hensley's driver chose the longer way to the docks, passing through the Port District construction area. "Progress," the mayor muttered, smiling at the cranes. They looked like looming gallows in the thick fog, suspended monuments to a city that didn't know it was being led to slaughter.

Under the cover of darkness, Hensley arrived at an unmarked warehouse on the outskirts of town. The air inside was thick with tension, laced with the kind of silence that came from men used to hiding atrocities in plain sight. Only his most trusted lieutenants awaited him, their faces tight with expectation.

"Mr. Hensley," Morales greeted the man at the head of The Ring, his voice crisp, respectful, but edged with the alertness of someone always ready to obey or survive.

Hensley stepped forward, shedding his public persona like an old coat. His voice was colder now, devoid of its earlier warmth, honed sharp like a scalpel. "Report."

Evan Kane flanked Morales to his left. Evan was one of the mid-level enforcers of The Ring. He had a reputation for particularly heinous acts toward women, for taking liberties with the merchandise and not always leaving them exactly whole. His presence alone was a silent reminder of the organization's cruelty and its lack of boundaries. Evan stepped up and handed Hensley a tablet displaying spreadsheets and logistics reports, coded details of recent shipments and payments.

"The new routes through Eastern Europe are secure," Evan said. "But there's been chatter about cops sniffing around." His voice was casual, almost amused, as if the threat of exposure were just another game.

Hensley's lips pursed. "Cops?" he shot a look at Morales, the sharpness in his gaze cutting through the room. "Don't we have someone for that?"

Morales quickly retorted, "There's no problem, Mr. Hensley. It's taken care of." His voice was calm, but a flicker of tension betrayed him.

"Handle it," Hensley snapped. "We've come too far to let amateurs disrupt our work." His words hit like a whip crack, final and unarguable.

Tracey Block, another of The Ring's lieutenants, hesitated before speaking. "And what about the reporter? The YouTuber? She's been asking questions about your ties to some offshore accounts."

Tracey was an unassuming man, completely bald, standing around five foot five. He maybe weighed one hundred and sixty pounds. Tracey had worked his way through the organization with good old-fashioned double-crossing and backstabbing. He was not one to trust, but he was smart enough to stay alive.

Hensley smirked, a chilling expression that hinted at his ruthlessness, more reptile than man in that moment. "Send her a message," he said simply. The air shifted, colder now, as if everyone understood what kind of message that would be.

Turning to Morales, Hensley asked, "Is everything ready?"

"Right this way, Mr. Hensley."

Morales led him from the main building into another, a small, concrete structure with a NO TRESPASSING sign out front, weather-worn and ignored by the kind of people who didn't need warnings.

They walked into a small, dimly lit room. There was no light source save for the flickering fluorescent bulb overhead that buzzed faintly, casting long, twitching shadows across the stained concrete walls. The air was damp, thick, and heavy.

At the center of the room stood a steel chair bolted to the floor, its occupant trembling, hands bound behind his back with zip ties that bit into his skin. His face was bruised, a deep cut above his eyebrow dripping crimson down his cheek.

The door creaked as Hensley walked in. His polished shoes clicked against the concrete floor with precise, unhurried steps. He didn't look at the man tied up; his gaze was fixed on the table beside him, where an array of tools lay neatly arranged, pliers, knives, a blowtorch.

Each one gleamed under the flickering light, as though waiting their turn.

"Do you know what disappoints me most about you, Carter?"

Hensley spoke to the man as he slowly took off his suit jacket and handed it to Morales. His voice was calm, almost soothing, like a father chastising a child. A strange gentleness wrapped around the words, which only made them more unsettling.

He reached for a pair of latex gloves and slid them on with practiced ease. "It's not your failure. Failure can be forgiven if it's paired with loyalty. It's your carelessness. You left loose ends."

Morales took Hensley's coat and walked to the edge of the room, positioning himself just out of the immediate blast radius. He turned to observe, arms folded, stomach tight.

He never understood why Hensley liked to do this kind of thing himself. They had guys for this. Professionals. Specialists. But Hensley really did seem to enjoy it.

Morales had watched men kill out of anger or greed before, but Hensley did it like someone working on a crossword puzzle, calm, focused, and almost enjoying it. Each action calculated. Deliberate. Personal.

It made him shudder to think what Hensley might do to him if he screwed up. Even more reason to always have a contingency plan. A clean exit. A burner car. A backup identity. A plan to get out in a hurry if he had to.

Hensley circled the chair like the leader of a wolf pack before dinner. Carter tried to speak, but his swollen lips barely moved. "I, I swear… I didn't mean,"

Hensley raised a hand sharply, cutting him off mid-sentence. "Intentions don't matter in my world."

He crouched down to meet Carter's eye level, his piercing blue eyes cold as ice. "You jeopardized everything I've built, the alliances, the deals... my legacy. And for what? A moment of weakness?"

Carter's breathing quickened as Hensley picked up a pair of pliers from the table and tested their grip with a sharp snap.

"Please... Mr. Hensley... I'll fix it! I'll make it right!" His voice cracked with desperation.

Hensley chuckled softly, a low, chilling sound that sent ice down Carter's spine. "Fix it? You think this is something that can be fixed?"

He stood up straight and paced slowly around the chair, like a predator circling its prey.

"No, Carter. Mistakes like yours don't get fixed, they get erased."

The blowtorch hissed as Hensley ignited it, its blue flame casting eerie shadows that danced across his face.

Carter thrashed against his restraints, panic overtaking him now. "No! Please! I have a family! My daughter, she needs me!"

Hensley paused, tilting his head thoughtfully. "Oh, that's right, Mara, is it?" His voice held a mocking calm, as if weighing the plea.

He glanced at Morales in the corner, then smiled, a cruel twist of lips devoid of humanity.

"Maybe we'll pay Mara a visit and bring her into the business. We could always use more merchandise."

Horror contorted Carter's face as Hensley brought the blowtorch closer to his skin.

The screams filled the room, then gradually turned to whimpers as Hensley worked, calmly, meticulously, not out of rage or impulsiveness but with cold precision.

After what surely felt like an eternity to Carter, Hensley finally set down the torch and wiped his gloves clean with a handkerchief before tossing it onto the floor beside Carter's limp body.

He leaned in close one last time to whisper in Carter's ear:

"This is what happens when you forget who holds your leash."

Hensley straightened his tie and walked toward the door without a second glance at Carter, or what remained of him.

He accepted his jacket from Morales as they passed three women hurrying by, followed by a burly enforcer tasked with cleaning up the mess.

Outside, the fog crept in thick over the docks as Hensley's Escalade V slid quietly into the night, his dual lives perfectly compartmentalized, for now.

Hensley hummed along to the catchy song playing on the stereo, Carter's screams still echoing faintly in the warehouse behind him.

CHAPTER 7: FISHING EXPEDITION

Colt's first move was to gather intel on one of Beemer's last known locations. He didn't get much from Tally; what he did find was a seedy bar operating on the south side of St. Pete. Colt also picked up a few fragments of Beemer's investigation from a YouTuber she'd been following, one who went by November Collins.

Colt knew he couldn't do this alone. He reached out to his old SWAT partner and sniper spotter, Marcus "Bear" Bennett. If he didn't include Bear in this, Bear would have his hide. Bear had earned his nickname in the Army, not for size, but for carrying an enormous load. Colt was particularly impressed with how well Bear did on the sniper assessment. Colt had held the record for the dreaded 100-yard low crawl through the briar patch, until Bear's tryout. Since then, they'd argued nonstop about who was faster, always planning a "crawl-off" to settle it once and for all.

Bear and Beemer were close. They'd joined the department around the same time, were about the same age, and both were war veterans. Bear was fresh out of the Army, only a few years into the department. He and Colt were cut from the same cloth, quiet but sharp, and they clicked instantly.

"I hadn't heard from her in over a week; I was starting to get worried," Bear said.

"How the hell did you get involved? I thought you were retired?"

"I am retired," Colt retorted. "I got a phone call out of the blue…"

Colt filled Bear in on all the details.

They began surveillance on the nightclub nestled in the heart of downtown South St. Petersburg. Both Colt and Bear had used 'urban camouflage' before in sniper operations, blending in so they wouldn't get called out as cops, retired or otherwise.

Outside, a neon sign flickered erratically, casting a sickly green glow over cracked pavement. The bar, simply named Wilson's Lounge, was a haven for the desperate, the dangerous, and the damned. Colt and Bear exchanged a glance as they stepped through the grimy door, their faces masks of careful composure shaped by years of dealing with people like this.

Inside, the air hung heavy with cigarette smoke and the stale stench of beer. A jukebox in the corner wheezed out Steve Earle's "Copperhead Road," barely audible beneath murmured voices and clinking glasses. The patrons were a motley crew, tattooed bikers, shady figures hunched over their drinks, and a few women with hollow eyes that spoke of sleepless nights. Their boots seemed glued to the floor, as if the place refused to let them go. The jukebox coughed up another warped tune, battered by years of smoke and dust.

The bartender, a wiry man with a scar tracing down his cheek, glanced up as they approached. His eyes narrowed briefly, but his expression stayed neutral. "What'll it be?" he asked gruffly.

Colt leaned against the counter, eyeing the poor selection. His voice casual, "Milagro tequila, rocks." He nodded toward Bear. "He'll take a Jameson."

Colt grabbed their drinks and carried them to a small table tucked in the corner, one that gave a clear view of every entrance and exit. They settled in, sitting for what felt like hours, eyes sharp. They played the part of patrons just drinking and passing time, but in reality, they savored their drinks slowly, watching, aware that with every hour, Beemer's trail could grow colder, harder to follow.

By his second drink, Bear's knee was bouncing, restless. He leaned in, voice low and gravelly. "I've seen girls slip into that back room, ones who never come out the front. Whatever's going on, it's back there."

Colt's eyes narrowed as he scanned the room. "Yeah, and for muscle, there's Skull-Knuckles over there. Looks like he runs the show. His backup? Bellhop Elbows-Magee, ready to crack heads at a moment's notice."

Bear smirked, savoring the colorful nicknames. "And don't forget the Einstein Brothers lurking behind them. They've got that 'don't mess with us' vibe written all over their faces."

Colt leaned back in his chair. "We wait for an opening."

After several hours and several whiskeys, Bear's patience was wearing thin.

"What kind of opening? Nikki's been underground for over twenty-four hours, if your tipster's right. She could already be sinking deeper into hell. I'm not just gonna sit here waiting for some fancy invite!"

Colt exhaled sharply, tone clipped but steady. "I know, Bear. I know." His gaze flicked again to the back room as his fingers tapped rhythmically on the table, the tension mounting.

"Well, I'm not waiting around anymore," Bear said as he strode up to the bartender. "So, what's it take to get some action in the back room there?"

The bartender stiffened imperceptibly, his hand tightening on the glass he was polishing. He glanced over at Skull-Knuckles and gave him a subtle nod. Skull-Knuckles then looked toward Elbows. Elbows approached Bear, a wide grin spreading across his face.

"You boys lookin' for some action? Well, why didn't you say so? Follow me."

Bear glanced at Colt. "See? That wasn't so hard."

Colt shook his head, rose, and reluctantly fell in behind Bear.

They followed Elbows-Magee through the doorway into a dim, narrow hallway. Flickering fluorescent lights overhead buzzed like dying insects, casting jagged shadows along the walls. Behind them, the Einstein Brothers moved in lockstep, their heavy boots thudding ominously against the floor. The hallway opened into a cramped room, its air thick with the stench of oil and sweat. Crates lined the walls like silent sentinels.

"You boys are just in time," Elbows said, his voice slick with menace.

Colt and Bear exchanged a sharp, loaded glance, a silent conversation that spoke volumes. This wasn't good. Colt's gut tightened as the Einstein Brothers fanned out around them like wolves circling prey. From the shadows behind, Skull-Knuckles stepped forward, his hulking frame blocking the exit.

"I think you boys are in the wrong place," Skull-Knuckles growled, his voice low and gravelly, like rocks grinding together. He cracked his neck with deliberate malice as he advanced. "You've been sitting here for hours, hardly drinking. Who are you? You smell like badges or dead men. Or are you just idiots looking to get your asses kicked?"

Colt took in the odds, four against two. Bad math. Then, with a defiant smirk cutting through the tension like a blade, he said, "Well, I'll admit, it's been a while since I had a good ass-kicking."

Bear snorted despite himself, but the humor vanished the instant Skull-Knuckles lunged forward with a fist aimed at Bear's face.

Bear dodged just in time, the punch grazing his cheekbone. Chaos erupted immediately, four against two.

Skull-Knuckles charged at Bear with brute force while Einstein #1 swung a rusted chain at Colt's head. Colt sidestepped, grabbed the chain mid-swing, and yanked hard to throw his attacker off balance. With a sharp elbow strike to Einstein #1's jaw, Colt sent him crashing into a crate.

Bear grappled with Skull-Knuckles and Einstein #2 simultaneously, his movements precise but strained under their combined weight. Every time he blocked one attack, another roared in, a relentless barrage of fists and kicks. Einstein #2 was a brute with fists of steel; Skull-Knuckles, a calculating prizefighter.

Elbows-Magee seized the chance to attack Colt from behind with a crowbar raised high. Colt caught the motion in his peripheral vision and twisted just in time to grab the weapon mid-swing. With brutal efficiency, he drove the blunt end into Elbows' gut, sending him gasping to his knees. Then he swung it across Elbows' face, blood running down like war paint. Colt always loved using whatever he could find as a weapon.

The fight was savage and unforgiving. Colt delivered punishing blows, an elbow to a face here, a knee to ribs there, while Bear ducked under Skull-Knuckles' calculated punches and drove sharp kicks into his knee joint. But despite their skill and ferocity, they were outnumbered.

Einstein #2 pinned Bear against the wall with his full weight, taking the brunt of several haymakers, while Einstein #1 played dirty, kicking Colt wherever he found an opening: ribs, knees. Colt staggered backward. Blood dripped from Bear's split lip as he fought against Einstein #2's iron grip; Colt gasped for air, pain flaring through his chest.

The room buzzed with violence, grunts of exertion mingling with the clang of metal on concrete, but neither man faltered. Pain was an old friend; surrender wasn't.

With sheer grit and determination, Bear slammed his knee into Einstein #2's groin, dropping him to his knees. He spun, delivering an uppercut that sent Skull-Knuckles sprawling, unconscious on the floor.

Colt ducked under another wild swing from Elbows-Magee and grabbed an empty bottle from a nearby crate. In one fluid motion, he smashed it across Elbows' face, shards flying like deadly confetti.

Einstein #1 hesitated for a split second, long enough for Colt to seize control again. Moving like synchronized predators, Colt and Bear unleashed a flurry of punches and kicks, dropping their remaining attackers one by one.

Bear and Colt then returned to the kneeling, gasping Einstein #2 and finished him off with a barrage of punches that sent him crashing to the floor like King Kong from the Empire State Building.

Colt's lip was busted and raw. Bear's hands were a mess, red and swollen. The air hung heavy with sweat, fear, and something even worse.

Breathing hard but victorious, Colt grabbed Skull-Knuckles by the collar and dragged him into the corner. His voice was cold steel as he leaned in close.

"Come on, princess, we've got things to discuss."

CHAPTER 8: CLEANING THE CATCH

Colt wiped his split knuckles as he dragged the half-conscious Skull-Knuckles through the rear parking lot of Wilson's, each step sending fresh pain stabbing up his ribs. His boots crunched on broken glass and gravel, Bear covering their exit. The night was thick and heavy, the kind of darkness that pressed cold against your skin. Across the street, the neon sign of the hourly motel flickered, casting sickly green light over cracked pavement. They hauled Skull-Knuckles behind the building to a forgotten shack, windows boarded, door hanging crooked on rusted hinges.

Inside, moonlight slashed through broken slats in the walls, painting jagged stripes across the greasy floor. The air hung thick with the stench of sweat and old rot, so dense it felt like you could chew it. Colt dropped Skull-Knuckles onto his side; the man grunted as he hit a splintered post. Colt's knuckles were raw, blood seeping from split skin. His breath came in short, ragged bursts. I'm too old for this shit, he thought, flexing aching hands.

Bear loomed behind him, scanning for anyone watching. His gaze locked on the shadows, eyes darting, every muscle coiled.

"Hurry it up, Colt," Bear muttered, voice low and urgent. "We don't have all night."

"I didn't see you help drag this piece of meat across the street. Thought you were the one who could haul a ton?" Colt said plainly.

"I can haul my fair share, but you still got sixty pounds on me, buddy," Bear shot back.

Colt gave Bear a look that could strip paint as he crouched, his knees popping like gunshots, in front of Skull-Knuckles, who was barely conscious, his head lolling. Colt slapped him, not too hard, just enough to sting.

"Wakey-wakey," he said, voice rough like gravel.

Skull-Knuckles's eyelids fluttered. He groaned, lips split and bleeding. "The hell...?" he slurred. His breath came in wet, ragged gasps, each exhale flecking blood onto Colt's boots.

Colt grabbed the man's collar, hauling him upright until their faces were inches apart.

"Wake up," Colt growled, his patience was razor thin. "We want answers. Where do the girls come from?"

Skull-Knuckles spat blood at Colt's boot, defiant even   now. "Girls? What, you two wanna start a daycare?"

Bear shifted, impatience radiating off him. Colt shot him a look, then turned back, a cold smile curling on his face. Without warning, he drove his fist hard into Skull-Knuckles's solar plexus. The man's eyes went wide, a strangled cough tearing from his throat as he gasped for air.

Bear stepped forward, his shadow swallowing the battered thug. His voice was ice cold.

"I'm all rested and I'm tapping in. You're already leaking. Don't make us ask twice."

Skull-Knuckles wheezed, trying to suck in a breath. "You got nothing," he rasped, but the bravado was slipping. "You think you scare me?"

Colt leaned in, his tone deadly calm.

"You should be scared. 'Cause no one's coming for you. Not tonight."

Before Skull-Knuckles could answer, headlights swept across the walls, throwing everything into stark relief. Red and blue strobed through the cracks, sirens silent but the threat unmistakable. Tires crunched on gravel outside. Colt and Bear froze, eyes locking. Every muscle tensed, ready to bolt, or fight.

The door creaked open, hinges screaming. A uniformed deputy stepped inside, flashlight beam slicing through the gloom, gun already drawn.

"Hands where I can see 'em!" the deputy barked, voice sharp as a whip.

Colt's hands went up, slow and steady, his mind racing. Beside him, Bear did the same, eyes flicking to the deputy's weapon.

"No problem here, Deputy," Colt said, voice flat but steady, masking the adrenaline surging through him.

Bear's hand twitched near his concealed Sig P365 9mm in his waistband. How far would he go? One wrong move, and he might have to take drastic measures to save Nikki. He knew where his loyalty was, and what he'd do. Bear made his internal decision quickly.

The deputy's flashlight was blinding, pinning them in place. He hesitated, squinting. Then his tone shifted, suspicion giving way to something else. His light lingered on Bear's face.

"Bennett? That you?"

The air was thick, electric, one wrong twitch and this could go sideways.

"Uh, yeah... Who's that?" Bear tried to keep his voice even, but tension crackled in every syllable.

The deputy stepped closer, lowering the beam.

"It's me. Rob McCarthy. From the academy."

Relief hit Bear like a gut punch, but his hands stayed up. "Rob? Shit, man, you almost gave me a heart attack." His voice sounded casual, but his eyes never left the deputy's gun.

"Yeah, well, shit, Bennett, you tryin' to get shot?!"

McCarthy said plainly.

McCarthy's gaze darted between them, suspicion lingering. "What are you doing out here, Bennett? This some kind of undercover op?"

Bear forced a grin, sweat beading at his temple. "You know it. Wait, you're not recording, are you?"

McCarthy shook his head, flicking off the body cam with a nervous laugh.

"We just got these damn things. I always forget to turn them on."

Bear stepped closer, lowering his voice, urgency bleeding through. "Listen, this is my partner, Officer Flynn." He nodded at Colt, who managed a tight, fake smile.

"We're working on something. You want to help? You never saw us."

McCarthy's hand hovered near his holster.

"You want me to forget I saw you?"

Bear's voice dropped, almost pleading.

"Yeah. Please. We were never here."

McCarthy hesitated, the silence stretching. Finally, he   nodded. "Nothing but a routine patrol..."

The deputy began to walk away, smiling. He shot Bear a double shooter finger.

"You owe me, Bennett."

Bear clapped him on the shoulder, tension finally breaking.
"Thanks, Rob. Let's grab a beer sometime."

McCarthy backed away, eyes still sharp, voice hard.

"You got it. Stay out of trouble."

Voices crackled on the radio.

"Code four, code nine, it's nothing..." McCarthy said into his mic as he walked back to his cruiser.

As the deputy disappeared into the night, Bear let out a shaky breath, shoulders sagging. The danger had passed, for now. He turned back to Skull-Knuckles, who was watching with wide, fearful eyes.

Bear crouched, voice low and cold.

"Where were we? Oh, right. No one's coming to save you. And we've got all night."

Colt cracked his knuckles, looming over the battered man.
"So, you wanna talk? Or do we keep playing rough?"

Silence was stale on the floor. Only Skull-Knuckles's wheezing broke the stillness, the promise of violence lingering in the air, heavy as the Florida night.

Somewhere outside, a loose chain-link fence clattered in the wind like ghostly applause.

CHAPTER 9: THE COUNT

Alena Hernandez's days blurred into a monotonous cycle of fear and survival; each hour indistinguishable from the last. The apartment where she was held, always locked, reeked of stale air and desperation. She shared the cramped space with several other young women, their faces gaunt and eyes hollowed by exhaustion. The traffickers controlled every aspect of her existence: meals were sparse, always cold, and served at rigidly enforced times. Thick black plastic covered the windows, shutting out any hint of daylight or hope.

Every morning, a heavyset man named Viktor would unlock the door with a metallic scrape that made Alena flinch. He barked orders in a guttural voice. "Up! Move! You want to eat, you work. No work, no food." The threat was always implicit, but sometimes he made it explicit, leaning in close so she could smell the sourness of his breath. "Remember, we know where your family lives. One wrong move, and they pay."

Alena's hands shook as she tugged on her threadbare uniform. She glanced at the other women, Maria, whose lips were split from a recent beating, and Katya, who barely spoke anymore. They exchanged looks, silent messages of solidarity and terror. Any attempt at kindness was dangerous; just last week, Maria had tried to share a crust of bread, only to be dragged into the bathroom and left there for hours, sobbing behind the locked door.

At the nightclub, Alena was forced to serve drinks at first, but the demands escalated quickly. One night, a trafficker named Evan cornered her in the hallway, his voice low and menacing. "Tonight, you're gonna do more. No arguments." When she hesitated, his fist crashed into her ribs, stealing her breath. "You want to see your mother again? Then do what you're told."

The psychological torment was relentless. She was watched constantly, even in the bathroom. Every word, every glance, was monitored. If she so much as looked at a customer the wrong way, punishment followed. "If you try to escape, we know where your family lives," Evan would remind her, tapping his phone as if ready to dial a number she dreaded hearing.

At night, Alena lay on the thin mattress, listening to the muffled sobs of the others.

She pressed her fist to her mouth to keep from crying out, replaying memories of her family, her mother's laugh, her little brother's smile. Was anyone looking for her? Did they even know she was alive? The darkness pressed in, thick and suffocating. She counted the seconds between footsteps in the hall, bracing for the next outburst or order.

One night, Katya whispered through the gloom, her voice barely audible. "You think we ever get out?"

Alena hesitated, then whispered back, "We have to try. We have to survive."

A sharp rap at the door silenced them.

"No talking!" Viktor's voice thundered. The threat hung in the air long after he left.

Meanwhile, on the other side of town at one of the Ring's many locations, Nicole Beemer's heart hammered as she pressed her back to the warehouse's rust-scabbed wall, sweat trickling down her spine. The fluorescent lights above buzzed and flickered, drilling into her skull like a swarm of angry hornets. She fought to steady her breathing, fingers tapping nervously on the top of her boot. I gotta make something happen here, she thought.

Across the oil-streaked concrete, three girls huddled together, eyes wide and haunted, tracking every movement in the room. Jan Morales, all cold smiles and shark eyes, stood at the center, his presence radiating menace. His enforcers prowled the loading bay, boots echoing on the concrete. The air was thick with the stench of diesel and fear, a taste Beemer couldn't wash from her mouth no matter how hard she swallowed.

Suddenly, the steel bay door screeched open, the sound slicing through the tension. A new group of women stumbled inside, herded like cattle. They looked broken, filthy, bruised, hair matted with sweat and grime. One collapsed as an enforcer shoved her forward.

Beemer darted over, catching the woman before she hit the ground. "You okay?" she whispered, voice barely audible, eyes darting to the enforcers.

A fist shot toward her face.

"Back on the wall, bitch!" the enforcer snarled, hand cocked to strike.

Uncharacteristically, Morales took interest in this one. She seemed different. Normally, his immediate response would be similar to his enforcer's, but for whatever reason, it wasn't.

"It's okay," Morales's voice cracked through the tension. "She's just taking care of the merchandise." He looked thoughtfully for a moment. "She speaks English. Maybe we can use her for something else."

The enforcer looked at Morales, hesitated, then backed off, muttering under his breath.

Morales turned to Beemer, his smile was razor-thin. "Don't mind him. All muscle, no manners."

Beemer forced herself to shrink, to look harmless, invisible. "Thank you," she muttered, eyes downcast.

Morales's gaze lingered, calculating. "You speak English?"

"Yes," Beemer replied, voice trembling just enough to seem afraid.

He grinned, teeth flashing. "Okay, American. You'll do. I need someone to do the count for me. You can count, can't you?"

Beemer nodded quickly. "Yes."

Morales barked at one of his men. "Ash! Get her a notepad. She's doing the count. I want every number checked, then checked again. No mistakes."

Ash Mercer, Morales's favorite sadist attack dog, shoved a notepad at her, his eyes cold.

Morales looked at her. "Okay, let's see if you are as smart as you act. Write down how many girls you saw in the other room. Then, how many new ones came in just now."

Beemer feverishly scratched down the numbers from the other room, remembering the girls she saw as well as the ones that just arrived in the van. She then showed the notepad to Morales.

Morales looked over the pad, then glanced out into the other room and nodded his head in affirmation. "Okay, you're doing the count."

"Ash! See to it!" Morales barked.

Ash grabbed Beemer by the arm and walked her into the other room to begin the count. "Don't screw it up," he said.

Beemer swallowed hard, clutching the notepad. This was it. Her shot. If she played it right, she could map out the operation, and maybe, just maybe, get a message out. She prayed Tally had reached Colt. If not, she'd have to improvise. Too much was on the line to freeze now.

She took a breath, steeling herself. The clock was ticking, and in this place, hesitation was just another way to die.

She had a rough idea where she was, somewhere in the shadows of the port district, where secrets clung to every alley. But that wasn't enough. She needed answers: Where were the girls coming from? How did they end up here? Who was pulling the strings? Was this Morales the main guy? She had to figure things out.

Notebook clutched tight, Beemer walked through the warehouse beneath flickering streetlights, weaving among the women with practiced nonchalance. She kept her questions casual, her tone light, too much curiosity could get her killed. Ash wasn't a genius, but he wasn't a fool. He'd notice if she pushed too hard.

She sidled up to a girl with a swollen cheek, voice gentle. "Hey, are you hurt? Do you need water?"

The girl blinked, wary. "No... I'm okay."

Beemer scribbled a note, glancing over her shoulder. "If you need anything, just tell me. I'll try to help."

Ash's voice cut through the air. "What are you whispering about?"

Beemer straightened, heart pounding. "Just checking if she's sick. Don't want anyone getting the others sick, right?"

Ash grunted, suspicion flickering in his eyes, but he let it go.

Later, Beemer spotted Morales again, his face half-lit by the neon glow, and waved him down. "Hello, umm, sir!" Her voice was careful, almost too polite.

Ash's eyes narrowed, his voice a low growl. "What the fuck do you want?"

Morales raised his hand, silencing him. "It's fine, Ash."

Beemer pressed on, feigning concern. "Don't you think I should check on the girls? Make sure they're healthy? Last thing you need is an outbreak, right? I can handle it."

Morales studied her, suspicion flickering in his gaze. The silence stretched, thick as oil. After a tense pause, he nodded. "Alright. You do that. But don't take too long."

Beemer forced a smile, heart pounding. One step closer to the truth, if she played this right, she might just survive long enough to make a difference.

CHAPTER 10: MEET THE PRESS

Colt lingered outside the café in downtown St. Petersburg; shoulders hunched beneath a bright sidewalk sign. The rain had just stopped, but its memory clung to the air, thick and electric, puddles steaming as sunlight spilled back in. He scanned both sides of the street, eyes darting from corner to corner.

Old habits, he thought.

Inside, Amanda Collins sat alone in a corner booth, her battered laptop's glow casting sharp angles across her face. She looked up, eyes sharp and wary, as Colt approached, his boots squeaking on the damp tile.

"Amanda? Amanda Collins?" Colt's voice was low, rough, edged with suspicion.

Amanda's gaze flicked from his face to the door and back again. "Colt Flynn? You look just like your emails, total jock energy," she said, tone polite but measured. "Sit. Please." She gestured to the seat opposite, though her fingers hovered protectively over her keyboard.

Colt squinted at the comment. Was that a dig? he thought, sliding in, never taking his eyes off her.

"Your email was awfully vague. Are you a cop?" she asked, her voice just above a whisper, eyes narrowing slightly.

"Retired," Colt replied, his voice gravelly, the word hanging between them like a challenge. "You said you'd spoken to Detective Beemer. That you had information on the trafficking ring."

Amanda's lips twitched, almost a smirk. "Maybe. Depends, what's Beemer to you, Retired Officer Flynn?" She leaned in, her tone suddenly sharper, testing him.

Colt gave a concerned smile. "She's a friend. And I think she's in trouble." His eyes bored into hers. "I need to know what you know."

Amanda hesitated, then glanced around the café, lowering her voice. "I've been tracking a shipment, names, locations, dates. It's bigger than I thought. And it's moving fast. Too fast."

Colt leaned forward, voice barely audible. "How fast?"

"Last night, I got a ping. Cargo's shifting tonight. If I'm right, Beemer was onto something, something she shouldn't have seen."

Colt's gaze flicked past Amanda, noticing for the first time a man in a dark jacket in the far corner, pretending to read a menu but glancing their way too often.

Amanda followed his gaze, her voice dropping to a whisper. "You see him too?"

"Yeah," Colt muttered, fingers drumming on the table. "You know him?"

"No. But I've seen enough creeps to know when I'm being watched." Amanda closed her laptop with a soft click, her hands trembling just slightly.

Colt's tone softened, but urgency crept in. "You got anything that'll help me find Beemer? Anything at all?"

Amanda swallowed. "I've got addresses, data points... here, look." She slowly turned and slid the laptop toward Colt. On the screen was a map of the area with red dots clustered near the port. "There's a lot of action in these areas, some official reports, some from my sources."

Colt tried to focus on where the majority of points were, making mental notes.

Amanda pointed to a dot on the screen. "Here. A warehouse. But," She hesitated, glancing again at the man in the corner. "I don't know who to trust anymore."

Colt nodded grimly. "You trust me. For now, that's all you've got."

The two sat and talked for the next hour.

"Sooo, if I may ask, why do you want to help Detective Beemer so much? She doesn't even work at your old agency," Amanda inquired.

Taking a sip from his coffee, Colt began, "Ah, well, she used to. I trained her, actually. After fifteen years and over a hundred or so trainees, she was one of the few I didn't feel like killing at the end of the day." He smiled.

"Ahh, I see. That bad? Training recruits?" Amanda asked.

Colt's lips twitched, almost a smile. "You have no idea. Try to take someone off the street and teach them how to run toward gunfire instead of away from it," he said, voice gravelly. "Most people, they're not built for it. You take a regular guy or girl, maybe they've worked retail, maybe they're just out of college. First time they hear a shot fired, their instincts scream to duck and hide."

"So, what's the hardest part?" Amanda asked, voice low, careful not to draw attention from the other late-night patrons.

Colt shrugged, glancing out the door. "You can drill procedures, teach them to shoot, run scenarios until they're blue in the face. But you can't train out fear. Not really. All you can do is hope when the moment comes, they don't freeze. That they remember the badge means more than their own skin."

A siren wailed in the distance, echoing down the empty street.

Amanda's pen paused. "And if they don't?"

Colt's gaze hardened. "Then someone gets hurt. Or worse."

Amanda scribbled something, eyes never leaving his face. "But you did it. Over and over."

He leaned in, lowering his voice. "You want the truth? Half the job is fighting the city, the other half is fighting your own people's doubts. You're not just training cops. You're trying to build something solid out of fear and uncertainty. Sometimes it works. Sometimes it doesn't."

Amanda nodded, the weight of his words settling between them.

They spent the next hour trading information, Colt pressing for details, Amanda offering what she could, both glancing at the door whenever it creaked open. The man in the corner never ordered, never moved, just watched.

Just before they were about to leave, the suspicious figure in the corner quickly got up and exited.

When they finally stood to leave, Amanda's nerves were raw. "Walk me to my car?" she asked, voice tight.

Colt nodded, eyes scanning the café one last time. The man was nowhere to be seen.

They stepped into the alley behind the café, the brick streets worn from years of use. Amanda stopped dead, gasping. A crowbar jutted from her windshield, glass spiderwebbed around it. The man from the café lounged against the wall, lighting a cigarette, his face stoic.

"Well, ain't that a bitch," he drawled, announcing to apparently no one while exhaling smoke. "Maybe you shouldn't park where you don't belong, Miss Collins."

Amanda stiffened. "What do you want?"

He grinned. "The Ring sends their regards, and, oh yeah, stop digging." The man raised his cellphone and snapped a picture, presumably as proof for his employer, then turned to walk away casually, as if he'd just commented on the weather.

Amanda immediately grabbed her phone and began to dial 911.

Colt stepped forward. "Oh, hell no." Grabbing the man by the collar and spinning him around, he growled, "You do this?" His voice was ice, finger stabbing toward the ruined car.

The man sneered. "What the fu, ?! I'd back off if I were you, old man. You don't know who you're messing with."

Colt froze, then smiled, cold as a blade. Glancing at Amanda, he said almost conversationally, "He's right, Amanda."

"Cops are two minutes out," she said, phone in hand.

Then, without warning, Colt drove his fist into the man's gut. The thug doubled over, coughing, dropping to his knees. But as soon as he hit the pavement, his hand darted to his waistband, pulling a Glock 19.

Colt moved on instinct. He hammered the man's wrist with his right hand, then grabbed it. With his other hand, his fingers closed around the Glock. His shoulder screamed, old injury flaring. Gritting his teeth, he wrenched the gun free, brought it up, and in one fluid motion, using it like a hammer, brought the butt of the weapon down on the man's skull. The man hit the ground hard.

After a moment of gathering himself, the thug leered at Colt. "You just signed your death warrant, man!" he spat, voice hoarse.

Colt's fist snapped the man's head back, sending him sprawling.

Colt turned to Amanda, who stared wide-eyed.

Sunlight glinted off the shattered windshield like a warning.

"Come on," Colt hissed, grabbing her hand, eyes sweeping the street for more threats. "Cops will be here any minute."

"No, they won't," Amanda retorted. "Fake phone call."

"Fake phone call?" Colt echoed, incredulous.

"Seemed like you had it under control." Amanda smiled at him.

Looking back at her sideways, Colt said, "I am a little rusty, you know. Besides, that was a message. You're closer than you think. This just got a hell of a lot more dangerous. We need to go, now."

Amanda nodded, breath shaky. "Where?"

"Somewhere they won't find you," Colt said, glancing over his shoulder as sirens wailed in the distance. "And fast."

CHAPTER 11: THE WATER COOLER

Deputy McCarthy hunched over his desk. The fluorescent lights hummed like a swarm of locusts as he shuffled paperwork, busywork to keep his mind off the night before. Officially, nothing happened. No mention of Bear and Colt in the logs. But McCarthy had a mouth, and secrets never stayed buried long at this station.

He slid into a battered chair across from Deputies Vance and Mercer, their coffee steaming between them.

"You'll never guess who I ran into last night, Bennet," McCarthy blurted, voice low but eager.

Vance didn't look up. "Bennet from the academy?"

Across the room, half-hidden in the shadows near the evidence lockers, Detective Brandon Quinn listened. He looked like he was lost in his own world, fingers lingering on the notebook's edge, the same spot where he'd tucked last month's overdue bill.

McCarthy leaned in. "Yeah. He was deep undercover, running with some older guy from his department. Flynn, I think. They'd roughed up Benny Havens over at Wilson's, left him bleeding on the floor."

Mercer snorted, shaking his head. "No shit? Havens always was a bastard. What were Bennet and his partner working on?"

McCarthy shrugged, eyes darting. "Didn't say. Didn't want to get in their way, you know how it is."

Mercer barked a laugh. "Hell, feel free to clean up our garbage!"

Vance finally looked up, eyes narrowing. "Seriously, should've done us a favor and just taken Havens out. Save us the paperwork."

His tone stayed light, almost casual, but there was a sharpness beneath the humor, a subtle warning dressed in a grin.

McCarthy forced a laugh. It echoed empty, more reflex than amusement. "Yeah, maybe next time I'll hand them a mop and bucket. Anyway, I just wanna make sure if Bennet is gonna drag me into some shit, I deserve a heads-up, ya know?"

Mercer grinned, but his fingers betrayed him, tapping a nervous rhythm on the table. "Yeah, and Bennet's not the type to forget a face." He turned back to his computer, the glow of the screen catching the edge of his jaw. "And don't let the captain hear you talking like that. Last thing we need is Internal Affairs sniffing around again."

Vance leaned in, dropping his voice until it was barely more than a breath. "You think Bennet's in over his head? Or is he playing a bigger game?"

McCarthy's mouth twitched. He glanced toward the door, a flicker of instinct flashing across his face, like he expected it to swing open any second. "I don't know. But the way he looked at me, like he was warning me off. Like I was some problem he didn't have time to deal with."

Silence pressed in, the kind that settled behind your ribs and made breathing feel like a mistake.

Then Mercer broke it, letting out a chuckle that felt more like a release valve than humor. "Well, whatever it is, it's above our pay grade. Let's talk about something else. You catch the game last night?"

Their voices rose and fell like the tide rolling through a shipwreck, jagged, uneven. They swapped stories about bad calls and worse luck, splintered jokes cutting through the lull. But the laughter never quite reached their eyes. It was brittle, camaraderie stretched taut over a bed of quiet dread.

Detective Quinn keyed in on the name Flynn, the syllables tugging at a thread of memory. They'd crossed paths before, he was sure of it. You get involved with enough cases in the county over the years, that kind of overlap is inevitable.

But that was another life. He wasn't on the job anymore. Retired. Just a relic with a badge-shaped shadow.

Still, he listened closely, letting every word from the deputies carve itself deep into his memory. Wilson's Bar. Havens. Bennet. Flynn. The names echoed like loose rounds in a tin can, each one a potential bargaining chip.

Justice? Quinn had buried that concept alongside his second divorce. The department hadn't just broken him, it had hollowed him out. Years of chasing monsters blurred the lines. Victims, suspects... the faces melted together. Two ex-wives, a mountain of debt, and a city that took more than it gave. He didn't care how the bills got paid anymore.

He shut his notebook, lips curling into a thin, knowing smile. He knew exactly where to peddle intel like this for cold, hard cash. The city's underbelly was always starving, especially for whispers that came from someone who used to wear a badge.

The station felt colder now, the walls inching in, secrets bouncing off cinderblock and settling like frost in his marrow. Out here, trust was a currency, and Quinn was about to cash in, no matter who got burned.

CHAPTER 12: FIRST SHOT

Rain hammered the cracked pavement outside the shuttered pawn shop, neon reflections bleeding into puddles like liquid fire. Inside, the air hung heavy with the scent of old gun oil and mildew, the kind of smell that clung to your skin and settled into your bones.

Vic Shaw leaned against a battered display case, his gloved fingers tapping a slow, deliberate rhythm on the dusty glass. Each tap was a countdown. A warning. A promise.

The phone in his pocket buzzed, a coded text, terse and unmistakable.

Target confirmed: Two local UC cops. Eliminate.

Vic's lips curled into a humorless smile. He let the phone drop back into his coat, the buzz still echoing in his nerves. He already had the backstories.

Officer Marcus Bennet, by the book, sharp-eyed, always scanning for threats. Easy enough. A creature of habit.

The second, though, was a different story. Colt Flynn. His contact claimed he was undercover, still playing the game, but Vic knew better. He'd watched Flynn at the diner, seen the way he laughed with the owner, how he slipped a bill to the homeless vet out front without needing to be seen. This guy wore his badge like a faded memory.

Flynn had turned in his badge, burned out, broken by the job, stripped of the blue wall that once shielded him. A man with nothing left to lose.

Vic's mind swirled like a storm, calculations firing in cold, practiced rhythms. Bennet would be at the department tonight, routine, predictable, soft. The parking lot would be empty, shadows pooling beneath flickering lights like spilled ink. Vic could hit him there. Quick. Clean.

Or maybe stage a fake 911 call. Lure him into the open, then strike.

But Flynn was a different animal, restless, wired, always scanning angles. He'd seen Vic at the diner, eyes narrowing in quiet recognition. A silent warning. That kind of man didn't rattle easily.

Vic would need to catch him off guard.

Hit him where he felt safe.

At home.

He just had to grab his tools, a Beretta with a fresh mag, a pair of gloves. Nothing fancy. Just another job, he told himself.

But his pulse thudded in his ears.

A voice echoed in his mind, his handler's warning: "Don't underestimate Flynn. He's not like the others."

Vic smirked. "They all bleed."

Across town, Colt Flynn's house sat in silence, the kind that settles when the people who give it life are gone. Becca and the kids were out of town for the weekend, and the emptiness clung to the walls like fog.

Rain battered the windows, a steady, relentless drumming.

Colt poured himself a double of blanco Lalo tequila, the clear liquid catching the light like glass. He stood alone in the kitchen, the weight of solitude heavy on his shoulders.

He savored the first sip, letting it burn a clean path down his throat.

He muttered to himself, "Whiskey's for the old wounds. Tequila's for the new ones."

Whiskey was in his blood, Scottish and Irish roots running deep. But lately, tequila was his thing. Lighter. Sharper. A burn that matched the Florida heat.

People always asked him why. They didn't get it. Tequila wasn't some macho poison, it was clean, honest, no pretense.

He stood at the window, watching the rain blur the world outside, when movement snagged at the edge of his vision.

A figure, gun raised, the dull gleam of a suppressor catching what little light there was.

Shit.

Instinct took over. The glass flew from his hand, shattering against the wall in a sharp spray of shards as he dove sideways.

Suppressed shots thudded into plaster, muffled but deadly.

Colt scrambled behind the couch, heart hammering in his chest.

The front door creaked open, slow, deliberate, methodical.

Vic moved like a shadow, silent and precise, suppressor ready.

Colt's breath sawed at his throat. He scanned the room. Nothing but the old Martin acoustic six-string leaning against the wall, a relic from better days.

He called out, voice steady despite the adrenaline, "You picked the wrong house, asshole!"

Vic's footsteps were soft, predatory.

"You're not a cop anymore, Flynn. No backup. No badge. Just you and me."

Colt's fingers closed tight around the guitar's neck.

"I don't need a badge to put you down."

Vic rounded the corner, pistol up.

Colt swung the guitar with everything he had. Wood splintered; the Beretta spun across the floor.

Vic snarled, lunging for it, but Colt was already winding up a second blow.

Vic anticipated the move, countering with his forearm, glancing the makeshift weapon into his ribs instead of his jaw.

He trapped the guitar with his elbow and swung at Colt with his free arm, striking him on the cheek.

Colt grabbed Vic, locking his hands in place.

They crashed into the coffee table, shards of glass skittering across the floor.

Vic's fist connected with Colt's ribs, pain flaring white-hot.

Damn, didn't I just bruise those? thought Colt.

"You should've stayed retired," Vic spat, reaching for his ankle.

Colt saw the glint of metal and leather, back in the day, they called it a blackjack.

A short, bludgeoning device, sometimes used by law enforcement, sometimes by criminals.

Its design was simple: a heavy leather pouch, about ten inches long, filled with lead shot.

The blow came fast, slamming into Colt's temple.

Stars exploded behind his eyes.

He hit the floor hard, pain ricocheting through his skull.

His mind swam in a foggy haze.

Becca and the kids flashed in his thoughts, their faces flickering like ghosts in the chaos.

Then his father's voice cut through the confusion, sharp as ever:

"If someone's trying to kill you, make it really fucking hard!"

His mother's voice, softer, protesting:

"Jerry! Do you really have to swear?"

His father, gruff but loving:

"Darlin', for this lesson? Yeah, I do."

The memory snapped Colt back to reality like an electric jolt.

The images of his family drained away as adrenaline surged through his veins.

Survival instinct took over.

He shoved himself up with his left hand, his right already gripping the push dagger on his belt.

Two inches of double-edged cold steel. Colt always carried a blade somewhere on his person.

Vic loomed over him, eyes wild.

"You're finished, Flynn."

Colt's voice growled, "Not today."

His right hand plunged the blade deep into Vic's groin.

Vic screamed, stumbling back.

Colt was on his feet, driving the dagger into Vic's torso, again and again.

Blood sprayed in arcs, painting the walls.

Vic staggered, clutching himself.

Colt seized his head, driving his knee into Vic's face, once, twice, three times.

Bone crunched.

Vic sagged, but Colt wasn't done.

With a final thrust, he buried the push dagger in Vic's neck, severing his jugular.

Vic crumpled, blood spreading black in the lamplight.

Colt stood over him, chest heaving, adrenaline roaring through his system.

He whispered, "Make it really fucking hard...", his father's words a lifeline.

He stared down at Vic's body.

He'd killed before, Afghanistan, SWAT standoffs, always for a reason, always with distance.

This was different. This was personal.

The man hadn't been a faceless enemy or a hostage-taker in the crosshairs.

He'd come for Colt, deliberate, relentless, lethal.

The question gnawed at him: why?

Was it because of what he was working on?

Was it tied to Beemer?

Or was there someone pulling the strings, sending this assassin into his path?

Colt's replayed the moment in his mind, the flash of steel, the intent to kill in the man's eyes.

Whoever sent him had made a mistake.

They'd underestimated Colt's resolve.

One thing was certain: he wasn't going to let this go.

He'd find out who was behind it, and when he did, they'd wish they'd never crossed his path.

He knelt, searching through Vic's pockets, hoping for a clue.

A burner phone. A slip of paper. Anything.

He peeled back Vic's sleeves, looking for a tattoo. A scar. Nothing.

But this guy reeked of professional polish.

Private military? Cartel? Something else?

Colt's lips pursed.

He replayed the moment again, the flash of steel, the intent to kill in the man's eyes.

"Who sent you?" he muttered, voice raw.

The only answer was the rain, pounding against the windows, relentless.

Whoever it was, they'd made a mistake.

They'd underestimated him.

And now, he was coming for them.

Colt dragged Vic's body into the kitchen, blood smearing the tiles.

No time to clean, just enough to buy minutes.

He wiped the blood from his hands, grabbed his phone, and dialed a number he hadn't used in years.

"Bear. It's Colt. We've got a problem."

CHAPTER 13: THE BOYS

Colt didn't waste a second.

The corpse sprawled on his living room floor could wait, he had bigger problems.

His heart thundered in his chest, a caged animal desperate to escape.

He thumbed out a quick text to Becca: **Stay away from the house.**

A few days. Maybe more.

His hands shook as he hit **SEND**.

If they were bold enough to hit him at home, no one close to him was safe.

Bear could be next, at work, or anywhere.

He didn't know how much time Beemer had left, but he wasn't about to gamble with anyone's life.

He moved fast, muscle memory taking over.

Every step echoed through the empty house, bouncing off the walls and the silent, accusing corpse.

He snatched up his gear: his guitar case, not the battered Martin acoustic in the bedroom, but the case built for war.

It looked like a guitar case, but it really encased his custom M4.

He grabbed several pistols, a long rifle, a precision sniper rifle, his go-bag, and an all-weapons bag.

Everything slammed into the truck bed in under a minute.

He paused at the door, fingertips brushing the splintered wood where Vic's bullet had lodged.

The house felt different now, violated, haunted.

He glanced back at the body.

Whoever did this wanted him rattled.

They'd failed.

Colt hit the road, the engine snarling.

Headlights sliced through the darkness as he tore away from the curb.

He was already dialing.

This wasn't a one-man job anymore.

He needed backup.

He needed the boys.

First call: Tim Jackson. Federal DHS agent and former Marine, the kind of friend who brought the weight of the U.S. government to a fight. Tim knew the area, had cracked human trafficking rings before. Colt didn't know how deep this went, but someone had just put a hit out on a retired cop. That wasn't a warning. That was war.

Tim needed to know.

The phone rang twice before Tim picked up.

"Colt? It's late, man. What's,"

"Tim, listen. Someone just left a body in my living room. Professional job. I need you."

There was a pause, then the sound of rustling fabric.

"You hurt?"

"No. But they're bold, Tim. Too bold. This isn't a message. It's a declaration."

"Okay, I'll pull some satellite footage. If this is trafficking, DHS has eyes in the ports." Tim's voice dropped, all business. "Text me your location. I'll be there in twenty. You armed?"

Colt almost laughed.

"Locked and loaded. Bring the heavy stuff."

Tim grunted. "You got it. And Colt, watch your back."

They hung up. Colt could almost hear Tim's boots hitting the floor, the click of a loaded mag, the familiar rituals of men who'd seen too much.

Colt had met Tim by chance, two warriors recognizing each other in a crowd, unaware they shared mutual friends. By coincidence, they both realized they were basically in the same business. They became fast friends, bound by a shared warrior spirit.

Second call: Maurice "Mo" Bishop. Mo was old Army, with even older tricks. He had an affinity for jazz and liked to listen to the likes of Ron Carter and Frank Morgan while he worked. These days, Mo was a ghost in the machine, doing cybersecurity for Big Tech, ex-sheriff's department IT, the guy who could hack anything.

The phone barely rang before Mo answered, his voice smooth as a midnight sax solo. "Colt, what you need?" That was Mo.

"Doesn't matter. I need eyes everywhere. Someone just tried to make me a headline."

Mo whistled low. "Damn. You want me to run the cameras? Cell towers?"

"All of it. And Mo, if you find anything, you call me first. No one else."

Mo chuckled. Before Colt even hung up, his phone buzzed, a secure link from Mo, already tracking nearby license plates. "Oh, and Colt, don't get dead."

Colt managed a grim smile. "No promises."

Back in 2023, there was a huge cyber breach at a sprawling, $14 billion chained resort reportedly tied to an organized hacking group. They were holding data for ransom. Mo actually ID'd them and locked them out before it could go any further. No one saw him coming. That was what he did. Mo was the guy who picked up the phone at 2 a.m. on the first ring. People underestimated Mo. They only made that mistake once.

Third call: Benjamin "Ben" Callahan. Ben lived and breathed guns, the kind of guy who'd argue bullet grain over breakfast. He made the Five-Eleven guy at the gun show look like a Cub Scout clutching a flea market switchblade. No military stripes, no badge, Ben was pure civilian, just this side of a sovereign citizen. He didn't trust the government, didn't trust the system, and sure as hell didn't trust anyone who tried to tell him what he could or couldn't own.

Ben answered on speaker, static crackling. "Colt. You know it's after midnight, right?"

"Yeah, Ben. I need you. Full kit. This is bad."

Ben's tone sharpened. "How bad?"

"I just left a corpse in my house. I'm not waiting around for round two."

There was a long silence. Then, "I'll bring the toys. You want the RV?"

Colt hesitated, picturing the battered RV parked in Ben's backyard, its windows blacked out. Ben's mobile armory, comms, medical, supplies, enough firepower to storm the castle. "Yeah. Bring the RV. And Ben, don't tell anyone. Not even your prepper buddies."

Ben snorted. "You think I trust anyone? I'll be there in thirty."

But for all his paranoia and bunker mentality, Ben was the guy you wanted at your back when things went sideways. He was loyal, dangerously loyal. If you called, he answered. No questions. No hesitation. Maybe it helped that he had three massive gun safes bolted to the concrete in his den. Colt had only seen inside one of them, a museum's worth of firepower, meticulously maintained and catalogued. The other two were locked tight, secrets behind steel and code. Then there was the RV, of course.

With Ben, you never really knew where the line was between friend and arsenal. But when the night got ugly and the world turned mean, there was no one better to have in your corner.

Colt drove into the night, adrenaline burning in his veins, the city lights blurring past. Every shadow felt like a threat, every car in his rearview a possible tail.

The rules had changed.

Now it was his move.

And this time, he wasn't playing defense.

CHAPTER 14: MISSED OPPORTUNITIES

The warehouse office reeked of stale cigarettes, spilled Fireball whiskey, and the sour tang of fear. Jan Morales slammed the heavy metal door so hard it rattled the glass in its frame, the metallic clang echoing through the concrete bunker like a gunshot. The sound bounced off the walls, lingering in the thick, unmoving air, pressing down like a storm about to break. His three lieutenants, scared, and suddenly very small, snapped to attention, eyes fixed on the floor, as if the cracked linoleum might swallow them whole and save them from what was coming.

Overhead, a dying fluorescent bulb buzzed and flickered, spitting out sickly white light that carved jagged shadows across Morales's face, making his eyes look black and bottomless, like pits with no mercy at the bottom. He stalked across the room, boots pounding the floor with every step, each thud a warning, each step a promise. His hands trembled, not with fear, but with a fury so raw it threatened to break him apart from the inside out. The botched hit, a dead shooter in some suburban living room, gnawed at him like acid on bone. The kind of mess that brought cops swarming. The kind that sent everything spiralling if it wasn't handled now.

He spun on his heel, voice low and venomous. "You idiots. You absolute idiots." The words cut like a blade in the quiet. He let them hang there, thick with contempt, savoring the way they made Marco flinch like he'd been slapped. "What was this job? You send one of our guys into a soccer mom neighborhood and he ends up dead on the floor?!"

He stopped inches from Marco Cross, the youngest of the three, barely out of his teens. Marco's lip quivered. His throat bobbed with a swallow, and his eyes, wide and bloodshot, tried to hold Morales's gaze, and failed. The air between them was charged, crackling like static before a lightning strike.

Marco's voice was barely a whisper. "Mr. Morales, we got a tip from that detective at the S.O., Quinn, I think? This Colt Flynn's retired. Not even a PI. He's just been... poking around. He and some off-duty cop roughed up Benny Havens at Wilson's Bar last night. That's one of ours."

He didn't dare say more. Not when Morales's silence was louder than shouting. Morales glared at Marco, waiting for more, the weight of his silence pressing down like a held breath before a storm.

"Yeah, soooo, we figured we would just send in a quick gun and take care of it, ya know?" Marco's voice was thin, brittle, his attempt at casual landing somewhere between a plea and a whimper.

Morales's sneer twisted, his face a grotesque mask in the flickering light. "And now he's still out there, poking around, because you couldn't finish the job."

He let the silence stretch, let it coil around their throats. The tension in the room thickened until it was almost suffocating. The only sound was the frantic buzzing of the dying bulb, louder than their breathing.

He whipped around, pinning each man with a glare. "Who was the genius you hired for this?" His tone was ice, and it burned colder than a scream.

Marco interjected, too fast, too eager to shift the blame. "Sir, Vic swore Flynn was just some burnout… We didn't know about Bennett!"

Evan Kane cleared his throat, voice shaky. "Vic Shaw was one of our local guys, he's worked for us before, no problems. Always gets it done." He tried a shrug, but it looked more like a spasm than confidence. "Good reviews, you know?"

Morales's fist crashed down on the desk, scattering papers and sending a chipped coffee mug spinning to the floor. The sharp crack echoed like a gunshot in the small room. "Good reviews? You think this is Yelp, Evan? You think I care about five-star ratings?"

He paced once, just once, then stopped dead. "Now I have to go to him. The boss."

The words caught in his throat, bravado flickering for just a second, just enough for the others to see the crack in the armor.

"You think the boss cares about your excuses? About   your   reviews?" He leaned in, nose-to-nose with Evan, his breath hot and sharp, the scent of whiskey and rage curling in the space between them.

"He'll care that I failed. That The Ring looks weak. And you know what happens when The Ring looks weak, don't you?"

He waited, eyes locked on Evan like a predator watching for the twitch of prey. A bead of sweat slid down Evan's temple, slow and glistening. Morales watched it trace the curve of his face, watched the man's Adam's apple bob as he swallowed.

Evan's voice was a croak. "Yes, sir. I know."

Morales straightened, raking a hand through his hair, fingers catching in the tangles of stress. His chest rose and fell in short bursts, breath ragged, uneven. He could feel the rage slipping, the mask cracking, and underneath it, the cold gnawing fear clawed its way to the surface.

The boss didn't tolerate mistakes. Not from anyone. Especially not from Jan.

Morales's hands clenched, his nails biting into palms, until the sharp sting grounded him, tethering his fraying nerves.

He forced his voice steady, even though it felt brittle under the weight of the room. "So, who do we have to clean this up? Flynn's retired, but he's still dangerous. And who's the other one?"

Marco blurted out, "Uhh, Officer Marcus Bennett. Six years on the force. Ex-military, SWAT, sniper. He's... he's no joke either, sir."

Morales's eyes narrowed, calculating like a predator sizing up prey. "Two trained pros sniffing around our business. That's not a coincidence. That's a problem. We need to even the odds." He turned to Tracey Block, the only one who hadn't spoken. "Tracey?"

Tracey stiffened, voice barely above a whisper. "Yes, sir?"

"Call in the Shroud."

Tracey hesitated, eyes darting to the others as if searching for an escape that wasn't there. "Uh, umm, yes, sir. Right away."

Morales's lips curled into a cold, sharp smile. "You know what happens if the Shroud says no, Tracey? You know what happens if this gets back to the boss before we fix it?"

He let the question hang, unfinished, the threat more terrifying for its silence.

Tracey swallowed hard; his throat clicked painfully as he forced the words out. "I'll make the call, sir. I promise."

Tracey knew the implications. The Shroud didn't just kill targets. He cleaned house, including any screw-ups that came before him.

Silas Stroud, the Shroud, had carved out a deadly reputation on the West Coast: hits executed with surgical precision, zero collateral, no loose ends. If anyone could erase Flynn and Bennett, it was him.

Morales shrugged on his coat, voice dropping to a whisper so cold it made the room shiver. "Pray the boss blames me, not you. Because if he doesn't,"

He let the words trail off, unfinished, then stalked out, slamming the door behind him so hard the bulb overhead flickered and almost died.

Tracey's mind flashed to the last crew who'd disappointed the boss, bodies found with their own limbs stuffed down their throats.

The men finally exhaled, relief and terror tangled in the stale air. Evan wiped his brow, sweat shining under the flickering light. Tracey's fingers trembled as he pulled up the Shroud's burner number, one wrong digit, and he'd be the next loose end. Marco just stared at the cracked linoleum, trembling.

Outside, Morales paused, the night wind biting his face, the city's neon glow painting him in sickly colors. He squared his shoulders, but his hands still shook.

Facing the boss was worse than any cop, worse than any bullet, worse than death itself. And tonight, he'd have to do it alone.

CHAPTER 15: THE REAL PROBLEM

Just outside the warehouse office, on the cold, oil-stained floor, far enough from Morales's conversation with his lieutenants that their voices were a low, menacing hum, Beemer felt it. The shift. The static in the air. Something electric. Dangerous.

The tempo had changed, like the sudden silence before a gunshot. Something was about to break loose, and she could feel it deep in her bones.

The girls shuffled past, hollow-eyed and swaying, their footsteps scraping like dry leaves. Their handlers, thugs with dead eyes and restless hands, kept them moving, pumping them full of whatever it took to keep them docile.

Beemer tried to catch their eyes, tried to offer a flicker of reassurance, but most stared right through her. She'd been handling their "welfare", a sick joke, really. She'd used more Narcan in the last forty-eight hours than in her entire career on the street.

A girl stumbled, nearly collapsing. Beemer lunged, catching her just before she hit the concrete. "Easy, sweetheart," she whispered, steadying her. The handler, a bruiser named Manny, glared.

"Hands off. She's not your problem," Manny growled, his voice low and threatening.

"She's gonna be dead if you keep this up," Beemer shot back, her tone even. "You want Morales dealing with a corpse?"

Manny's lip curled, but he backed off, muttering under his breath. Beemer helped the girl to her feet, squeezing her hand gently, a silent promise.

Even Morales looked like he was about to snap. He paced inside the office, his voice rising and falling in sharp, angry bursts. Through the grimy window,

Beemer could see him gesturing wildly, his lieutenants, Evan Kane, Tracey Block, Marco, Ash, clustered around him like vultures. Beemer kept a running list of names, faces, threats. She'd memorized every detail. She knew the clock was running out for the girls. Which meant it was running out for her, too.

Her back hit the wall, each breath measured, in, hold, out, like training on the range. She needed to move fast. But what was the play? What had she missed? Three days underground, radio silence. Surely someone had noticed she was gone. Her team? Her department? She almost laughed at the thought. The department had its own Ring, only they called it the SuperPac. Unspoken, but real. They promoted their own, buried the rest. Good cops disappeared; careers snuffed out because someone in the SuperPac felt threatened. If the SuperPac could bury her career, they could bury this case too. No one was coming, except maybe Colt.

She remembered the last conversation she'd had with her partner, just before she went dark.

"You sure about this, Bee?" he'd asked, concern etched deep in his face.

"Don't have a choice," she'd replied. "If I don't go in, those girls don't come out."

He'd nodded, but she'd seen the fear in his eyes. Now, alone in the warehouse, she wondered if he'd even bothered to report her missing.

But her own issues aside, this was more important.

Florida ranked among the top three states for human trafficking in the U.S. Tampa, in particular, was a major hub for both sex and labor trafficking within the state. That was just a fraction of an estimated one hundred to three hundred thousand at-risk or trafficked individuals forced into sexual slavery in the U.S. each year. The numbers haunted her. She had to get out and do something, anything.

A sudden shout from the office made her flinch. Morales slammed his fist on the desk, sending a coffee mug flying. "If we get burned, it's on you, Ash!" he barked.

Ash's voice was cold. "No one's getting burned. I've got eyes everywhere."

Beemer edged closer to the door, straining to hear. The tension was thick, suffocating.

Then it hit her. Tally. Had Tally gotten word through to Colt? This had Colt's fingerprints all over it. The timing fit, Morales' panic, Ash's paranoia. Colt wouldn't sit idly by. If she got in touch, Colt would be coming. And if Colt was coming, she would have to be ready.

She had to formulate a plan. To move on a moment's notice when he arrived. Beemer strategized: if Colt stormed this place, they would use the girls as human shields, a distraction! A fire alarm? A fight with the girls? Anything to split their focus when it happens.

Suddenly, Ash appeared at the end of the hall, eyes sharp, suspicion etched across his face. "What are you doing?" he called out, his voice echoing off the concrete.

Ash had been watching her too closely, his gaze lingering like a blade at her throat. He was going to be a problem.

Beemer forced a smile. "Just checking on the girls. Some of them look rough."

Ash closed the distance, his shadow swallowing hers. "You're not here to play nurse. Get everyone in the office. Now."

Beemer nodded, heart pounding. She fell in line behind Ash, her mind racing. If she hesitated, she and those girls would vanish, just another ghost story whispered in the halls of the Ring. But now, at least, someone on the outside knew. And if Colt was coming, hell was about to break loose.

CHAPTER 16: THE DOUBLE CROSS

Sergeant Dane Sloane's office was a box of shadows and stale coffee. The city's neon pulse barely reached through the grime-streaked window, painting his desk with fractured light, urban bruises smeared across official reports. Sloane sat hunched, eyes fixed on the empty chair across from him, Detective Nicole Beemer's chair. Three days gone. Three days since she'd defied his order and vanished into the city's underbelly, chasing the human trafficking ring he'd told her to leave alone.

He drummed his fingers on the desk, the rhythm sharp and impatient, like a warning he couldn't quite hear. His phone buzzed, a coded message from one of the senior brass. "Update. Now." Sloane's stomach twisted. He owed them answers, not questions. And right now, all he had were ghosts and hunches.

He replayed their last conversation: Beemer's eyes, bright with anger, the way she'd leaned in, voice low, like they were conspiring, or confessing. "You know what's happening out there, Sarge. I can't just walk away. Container twelve, Sarge! Container twelve!" He'd barked at her, threatened to pull her badge. She'd walked out anyway.

Nicole had been his new bright and shiny star, sharp, relentless, maybe too much like him. If he was able to get her on his team, he would for sure make Lieutenant. Now the likelihood of that was looking less and less. And deep down, what scared him most wasn't the politics. It was the silence.

Now, he was the one left waiting. The silence pressed in, thick as guilt.

A knock at the door jolted him. Not Nicole, just Jenkins, the rookie, eyes wide and nervous. "No word yet, sir. Her last contact was a burner ping near the docks."

Sloane dismissed him with a jerk of his chin, his pulse thudding in his ears, louder now, like a drumbeat of inevitability. The docks, too close to the Ring's turf. Too exposed. If Nicole was alive, she was in the lion's den, and she knew everything.

And if she talked, if she found out what he'd done, what he was still doing, he'd be finished. Worse than finished.

There wouldn't be a badge left to bury.

He sat quietly and pondered his predicament, the weight of it pressing down like the cheap vinyl of his office chair. He thought back to how he first got involved with the Ring. He told himself it was a noble reason. His daughter was suffering, the department paid scraps, and the world didn't care about broken families in blue.

There was an opportunity, cash for just a little information. How much could it hurt? Just whispers. Nothing that felt like betrayal. Then he saw an opportunity to really help her, to pay for her surgery, all he had to do was look the other way. Just once.

Were there any real victims anymore anyway? Everyone had their hands out. Everyone had their secrets.

Sloane glanced at the flat-screen TV on the wall in the corner of the room…

"Breaking news with a developing story out of Pinellas County, from the Westside neighborhood, where authorities have launched an investigation into a body found inside the home of retired police officer, Colt Flynn. Authorities confirm the scene inside is nothing short of brutal.

"Neighbors reported suspicious activity before officers forced entry and walked into chaos, one corpse bearing the marks of a violent struggle. There's no sign of Flynn or his family. The home appeared ransacked, though officials have yet to confirm whether anything was taken.

"Flynn has not been seen or heard from since neighbors say they last saw him driving away from the scene in an expedited manner two days ago. He retired from the force just last year after a distinguished 25-year career marked by commendations and controversy alike…"

Police are urging anyone with information to come forward. As the investigation deepens, the question on everyone's mind: Where is Colt Flynn, and what was he running from?"

Sloane continued to concern himself with his own issues, letting the news anchor's voice blur into background noise. He wasn't really listening to the story on the screen or having any idea who Colt Flynn was.

Or did he?

Then it dawned on him, slow and sharp all at once. Where had he heard that name before?

Wait a minute, he had heard it from Beemer. Colt Flynn. That was the name. Her old FTO. She'd brought him up more than once, always with a strange tone, half-respect, half-regret. Could Colt have something to do with this? The timing felt too convenient. Too clean. Too coincidental.

He yanked open his desk drawer, his fingers brushing against the cold plastic of the untraceable burner phone, his last resort. His thumb hovered just above the number for his handler in Internal Affairs. One call, and the wheels would start turning. His skin prickled, damp with sudden sweat.

He needed Nicole found, but not by the wrong people. Not by anyone who'd ask the wrong questions. Not before he could get ahead of the story. Control it. Spin it, if he had to.

Was Colt Flynn involved with her now? Had they reconnected? Were they working together, or hiding together?

Outside, a siren cut through the air, distant but drawing nearer.

Sloane stared at the empty chair across from him, its silence accusing. A cold certainty slid into his chest and settled like lead: Nicole Beemer was either his biggest liability...

Or his only chance at redemption.

He had to find her first, before she ended up tagged and zipped in a morgue drawer, just another "retired" cop with no one to fight for her.

CHAPTER 17: RED TAPE

The rain drizzled steadily onto the cobblestones outside Flanagan's, turning the neon shamrock sign into a watery smear of green that bled across the sidewalk. It pulsed like a heartbeat in the puddles. Inside, the pub was a cocoon of shadows and old wood, wrapped in silence, its usual Friday night clamor replaced by something heavier.

Only four friends huddled at a corner table, their voices low, their shoulders tight. The air hung thick with unspoken words, and the acrid tang of spilled Guinness clinging to the floorboards.

Maggie O'Connell, the owner, met them at the door. Her sharp blue eyes swept the street one last time before she turned the lock with a heavy clunk. The sound echoed, hollow and final, through the empty room.

Flanagan's wasn't just a pub, it was their refuge. The walls, panelled with dark, worn oak, bore the ghosts of decades past. Each plank was etched with initials, hearts, and crude poetry scrawled by lovesick regulars long gone.

Above the bar, the shelves sagged beneath the weight of dusty bottles, Jameson, Bushmills, and a dozen forgotten Irish labels, each one whispering promises of comfort, confession, and a crushing hangover.

A row of mismatched pint glasses hung upside down, catching the warm, flickering glow of the stained-glass lamps overhead, as if waiting for a toast that might never come.

The floor was a patchwork of scuffed wood and faded tartan rugs, sticky in places where years of footsteps had worn the varnish down to bare grain. Every step gave a soft tack, like the place remembered every spilled pint and every stumble home.

In the far corner, a battered dartboard hung askew, its cork frayed and edges curled, surrounded by a constellation of errant holes in the plaster, trophies of inebriated bravado and forgotten wagers.

The jukebox, a relic from the seventies, crouched in its corner like a stubborn old storyteller. It hummed low, its neon lights flickering in sync with the thunder rolling through the sky outside, as if even the storm had a rhythm to share.

Maggie approached the friends, her boots whispering across the tacky floor. Her accent, as thick as the peat bogs back in Galway, wrapped around her words with warmth and iron. "Colton filled me in on your poor friend, Nikki," she said, voice low but steady. "You boys have the place to yourselves tonight. No one's getting through that door unless you say so."

She gave a nod, more promise than permission, before disappearing into the back office, the door swinging shut behind her with a soft creak.

Colt had called ahead and filled Maggie in on their needs for the evening. She then moved behind the bar with familiar ease, but when she set the glass down, her hand trembled, just enough for the men at the table to notice.

"I know the looks in your eyes, boys," she said quietly, eyes sweeping across their tense faces. "I've seen it before, men with a job to do, and no good choices left."

She paused, her voice softening, dropping to something near a whisper.

"Before you start, let me tell you something."

She didn't look at them, her gaze dropped to the worn wood of the table, and her fingers traced the grain like it was scripture.

"My niece, Siobhan, was taken three years ago. Just sixteen. Gone from the streets of Dublin in the blink of an eye. The Garda said she'd run off, but I knew better." Her voice caught, but she pushed through. "I've heard nothing since. Not a word. Most likely, she was sold, like cattle, into slavery somewhere far from home."

Her eyes glistened, but her jaw was set like iron. "That's why I keep this place open. For people who need a safe harbor. For those who fight back."

She met each of their eyes, one by one.

"Whatever you're planning, know you're not alone in it."

A heavy silence settled over the table, the kind that carried more than grief, it carried resolve.

Outside, thunder rolled, distant but steady.

Inside, something shifted.

Flanagan's wasn't just a pub tonight, it was a war room. And Maggie? Maggie was more than just a keeper of pints.

She was the kind of ally you didn't take for granted.

Before Maggie exited to her back office, she stopped just shy of the swinging door and reached into her apron. Without a word at first, she pressed a small flask into Colt's hand. It was worn silver, etched with a shamrock and the Gaelic blessing, "Go n-éirí leat."

Maggie looked deeply into Colt's eyes, the weight of her own memories swimming just beneath the surface.

"It's Siobhan's birthday next week... bring your Nikki home, Colton."

Then she turned and disappeared behind the door, leaving silence in her wake, heavy and holy.

Colt stood there, motionless for a moment, the echo of her footsteps still lingering in the dim hush of the bar. He turned the flask in his hand, the cool metal pressing into his palm, a small, secret comfort with a history of rebellion and solace, a ritual as old as regret.

Unscrewing the cap, he inhaled deeply. The sharp scent hit like truth, cutting through the fog in his mind.

"Ahh, the good stuff," he muttered, but even he didn't believe it.

Not yet.

Not until it's over.

His gaze drifted to the doorway where Maggie had vanished, the air still trembling with the weight of her absence.

How many doors had closed because of this? How many lives had been nudged off course, rippling outward in ways he couldn't see, or fix?

The flask felt heavier now, not just with whiskey, but with memory, each sip a silent tribute to choices made, and debts still unpaid. A quiet eulogy in silver and spirits.

He returned to the bar and set his Jameson down hard, the glass ringing against the oak, sharp and final. Overhead, the bulb sputtered, shadows twitching across his face like something trying to claw its way out.

He couldn't insult Maggie by ordering tequila. Not here. Not now.

He kept glancing at the window, half-expecting trouble to crawl through the rain-smeared glass, slick with city grime and unanswered prayers.

The mood was thick with old whiskey, nerves, and the unspoken dread that something, somewhere, had just gone terribly wrong.

Tim lounged against the bar, arms folded, drinking a Guinness, his badge half-hidden beneath a garish Hawaiian shirt. He tapped his foot, the metal of his holster clinking softly. All the men were armed tonight.

"You look like hell, Colt," he muttered.

Colt looked up from his glass, a big smile spreading across his face.

"Well, thanks, Tim. Good to see you too."

Mo hunched over his laptop, the screen's glow painting his face ghostly blue. His fingers drummed a frantic rhythm as he sipped a single malt neat.

"I've got chatter, but nothing solid. I'm still tracing your girl's last comms. She's not just off the grid, she's wiped it clean."

Ben built a fortress of gear, radios, vests, and ammo boxes, like a soldier prepping for D-Day, taking shots of Jameson between. He periodically glanced at the door every few seconds.

"We're burning daylight, Colt. If they've got her,"

Colt stopped pacing. His voice was gravelly.

"Beemer's gone dark. Last ping was two days ago, deep in the docks. She's embedded with the Ring. Human trafficking, guns, the works. If we don't move, we lose her."

Tim straightened, eyes narrowing, setting his half-empty glass of Guinness on the bar.

"The Ring? Jesus. That's not a crew you poke with a stick. I'll call in a few favors, see what my guys have. But if we go after them, we're not getting a parade when it's over."

Mo didn't look up.

"Names, numbers, burner phones, give me anything. I'll find her trail. If she left even a breadcrumb, I'll dig it out."

Ben zipped up a duffel, checking the contents with military precision. "I've got encrypted comms, range: two miles. Battery: twelve hours. And yes, they're bulletproof. I got extra vests, enough gear for a small war. But if this goes sideways, we're ghosts. No backup. No cavalry."

The door creaked. Maggie poked her head in, eyes darting. "Boys? Someone else here for you." Her voice dropped to a whisper. "This one looks like trouble."

Colt nodded.

"Send him in, Maggie. And lock the door behind him."

Bear Bennett stepped inside, rainwater dripping from his jacket. He carried a long rifle case and a backpack that looked like it weighed three times his own. His eyes swept the room, sizing everyone up.

"Bear," Colt said, his tone introducing both a man and a weapon. "He's new, but he's solid. Knows his way around a fight."

Tim stepped forward, extending his hand.

"Glad to have you, Bear. Just know, once we open that case, we're committed. Surveillance, manpower, legal cover. But if it all goes to hell, we're on our own."

Bear's grip could've crushed coal into diamonds.

"I'm not here for glory. I'm here to get Nikki back.

Whatever it takes."

Mo finally looked up, peering over his readers, sizing Bear with a quick glance.

"You got anything for me? Names, numbers, emails? I'll hack what I need. If she's out there, I'll find her."

Bear shrugged off his pack, setting it down with a heavy thud that echoed in the cramped room.

"I brought some toys. Some bangs. And a few tricks."

He cracked open his rifle case, revealing his personal Accuracy International AXSR .308, a beast of a rifle, its matte finish broken only by the gleam of the mounted optic and the folded stock. With practiced ease, Bear popped open the bipod and set the rifle on the table, the legs locking into place with a satisfying click.

He unzipped his bag and began unloading a small arsenal of tactical gear. Out came a compact suppressor, a thermal scope attachment, and a quick-adjust rear butt spike for rapid elevation changes. He set aside a pair of noise-cancelling comms headsets and a ruggedized tablet loaded with satellite maps and ballistic calculators. Next, he laid out a selection of smoke grenades, flashbangs, and a pair of breaching charges, just in case the night called for more than subtlety.

A Black-Hawk drag mat was rolled out for prone shooting, followed by a lightweight ballistic vest, a set of Kevlar gloves, and a gas mask. Bear's gloved hands moved methodically, arranging each piece of equipment with the calm certainty of someone who had done this a hundred times before. Finally, he checked the spare magazines, loaded with match-grade .308 rounds, and clipped a combat knife to his belt.

He glanced up, a wry grin tugging at the corner of his   mouth. "Never know what you'll need when things get loud."

Ben grinned, scanning Bear's gear, but his eyes were wary. "Bear, huh? You don't look much like a bear."

Bear cracked a rare smile and shrugged his shoulders. "Didn't pick the name."

Ben smiled.

"Yeah, well, looks like you earned it," he said, gesturing toward all the gear in front of him. Walking back to his own bag, he added, "Alright, Bear-Cub.

Let's see if you can keep up."

Then he addressed the group, voice low and steady.

"We go in heavy; we come out together. No one left behind."

Colt looked around the room and raised his glass. "Fides, Amicitia!"

All the others raised their glasses in unison.

"FIDES, AMICITIA!"

Bear, not fully understanding the gesture, followed suit. "Fides, Amicitia!"

A heavy silence settled. The rain outside intensified, drumming against the roof like distant gunfire.

Colt downed his whiskey and slammed the glass on the bar. He then looked at everyone intensely.

"I love you guys. I appreciate you all being here. We move out at first light. Mo, you're our digital eyes. Tim, get us what you can, warrants, backup, dirt. Ben, gear us up. Bear, you're on point with me. We find Beemer, we burn the Ring to the ground. No mistakes. No mercy."

Mo's screen lit up with a map, red dots clustering near the docks. "Beemer's last ping was here. But these heat signatures… that's a lot of bodies."

"I've got a drone on standby. But if we use it, my boss'll ask questions we can't answer," Tim stated honestly.

"You sure about this, Colt? We're not just poking the bear, we're kicking the whole damn hive."

Colt's looked at him.

"We don't have a choice. Beemer's family. These guys came at me at my house. It's only by God's grace that Becca and the kids weren't home. Sometimes you gotta just ride the darkness, brother."

Mo chimed in, "I got the drone covered."

Ben shot, "As far as I'm concerned, the Ring's about to learn what happens when you take one of ours."

Mo's fingers hovered over the keyboard.

"I'll keep eyes everywhere. If anyone so much as sneezes in the docks, we'll know."

Bear checked his rifle case, eyes cold and determined.
"Let's make sure we're the only ghosts walking out of there."

Ben snapped his duffel shut.

"First light, then. No turning back."

The bulb flickered again, shadows dancing across the walls. Outside, thunder rolled over Dunedin. Inside, the hunt had already begun.

CHAPTER 18: THE SHROUD

Silas Stroud was a man forged on the ragged outskirts of civilization, the bastard son of a nameless drifter and a mother who vanished before he turned eight. The world had never given him a soft landing. Foster homes and alleyways became his classrooms, teaching him the first rule: survival meant blending in, trusting no one, and never letting your guard drop, not even for a heartbeat.

He remembered the night the world showed him its teeth. Rain hammered the corrugated roof of the apartment where he hid with his only friend, Tommy. A scream, a flash of steel, and then silence. Tommy's blood pooled on the filthy floor, and Silas learned the second rule: attachments were weaknesses, and weakness got you killed.

He became a ghost. Never seen, never heard, never leaving evidence. His name was a warning, whispered with fear and respect in the underbelly of cities that pretended not to know him.

"Stroud's in town," someone would mutter in a trembling voice, eyes darting to the shadows. "Best keep your head down."

"Is he real?" another would ask, voice barely above a whisper. "Real enough to make you disappear," came the reply, cold and certain.

Military discipline. Government secrets. Black ops. Wetwork. Each step took him deeper into the abyss.

Each job stripped away another layer of humanity, leaving behind something sharper, colder. Contract killing was never about the money. It was about control, about erasing the chaos that had once ruled his life. Meticulous, cold, and always gone before the bodies hit the ground, Silas left nothing behind but questions and fear.

Now, they called him the Shroud. When the locals failed, when the job was too dirty for anyone else, they brought him in. This time, the contract was simple, at least on paper: eliminate two cops. One target was retired, a loose end. The other? Active duty, still on the force, with friends in high places. Both dangerous.

The client's voice crackled through a burner phone, low and urgent. "You understand the terms?" the voice asked.

Silas's reply was a whisper, barely audible. "Names.

Locations. That's all I need."

"You don't care why?" the voice asked. "We already missed the one , "

Silas cut him off, "Names. Locations."

The system had no record of him. No fingerprints. No face. Just a whisper in the dark. Haunted by the past but never ruled by it. Silas wasn't a sadist or a psychopath, he was a man broken in all the right places, channelling his damage into a cold, precise purpose. Redemption, if it existed, was something he found in the work , one trigger pull at a time.

He moved through the city like a rumor, eyes always scanning, ears tuned to the static of police radios and the rhythm of the streets. He watched his targets from a distance, cataloguing every habit, every weakness. In a dimly lit bar known for being a cop hangout, he silently listened to two off-duty detectives as they nursed their whiskeys, hands trembling just enough to betray old wounds.

"You hear about Flynn? Dude's got a target on his back," the one asked his companion, voice rough.

"You kidding? It's all over the news. Didn't he just retire? So much for enjoying that pension," his friend answered.

"I don't know, makes ya think. You ever get the feeling someone's watching you?" he asked again, quieter this time.

His friend laughed it off. "You're paranoid, Frank. Nobody cares about old cops like us."

Frank's eyes flicked to the window, catching only his own reflection. "Somebody cared about him… That's what scares me."

Silas inhaled their fear like smoke, savoring it, studying it. He took it in as if learning something from it, cataloguing the tremor in their voices, the darting eyes. He wondered what they had seen. How easy it would be to kill the two of them. But then again, they were not his targets.

An expert marksman, Silas adjusted the scope on his rifle, the crosshairs settling over a photo of Colt, taken from three blocks away, through a rain-streaked window. Silas spoke in multiple tongues and thought in patterns. Surveillance. Counter-surveillance. Digital forensics, he owned them all. He could slip through locked doors, vanish into crowds, erase himself from cameras and memories alike. Two local cops? They wouldn't even see him coming.

The city itself seemed to hold its breath as he moved. Every step, every glance, calculated. Every shadow, a possible threat. He trusted no one. Not even the woman who passed him on the street, her eyes lingering a second too long.

When the job was done, when the city woke to the news of two more dead, no evidence, no suspects, Silas Stroud would vanish again. Just a rumor. A shadow. A name passed between hushed voices by those who understood one brutal truth: monsters sometimes wear the faces of men.

And somewhere, in the quiet spaces between heartbeats, he would wonder, would the next trigger pull set him free... or drag him deeper into the cold, silent dark he'd come to call home?

Some nights, he still felt Tommy's blood on his hands, sticky, warm. It clung like memory. No amount of scrubbing ever washed it away.

CHAPTER 19: ALL THINGS MUST COME TO AN END

Jan Morales stood outside the heavy oak door, hands slick with sweat, heart thundering so loud he was sure Victor Hensley could hear it through the walls. He wiped his palms on his jeans, but it did nothing to steady the tremor crawling up his spine. The city's mayor, and the hidden boss of The Ring, waited on the other side, his shadow stretching long over every corner of Jan's life, dark and inescapable.

The failed assassination attempts on the one snooping around the business replayed in Morales's mind, every second sharper, louder, like glass breaking in his memory. Each mistake clung to him like smoke. Now, he had to report failure to the most dangerous man he knew, and he didn't know if he'd walk back out.

He hesitated; his fingers hovered over the wood. Should he knock? Should he run? His legs tensed with the thought. Before he could decide, the door swung open, almost as if Hensley had been standing there the whole time, hand on the knob, waiting for Morales to summon the courage, or to lose it.

"Come in," Hensley said, voice low and smooth, but with an edge sharp enough to slice. It made Morales's skin crawl.

The office swallowed him whole. Polished marble floors, cold as a morgue slab, gleamed beneath harsh overhead lights. Glass walls showcased the city skyline, cold, distant, untouchable. Everything about the room screamed control. Hensley sat behind a massive desk, his high-backed chair framing him like a throne. His fingers were steepled, his gaze unreadable, eyes like black ice.

Morales swallowed hard; his throat was sandpaper. He opened his mouth, but the words caught behind clenched fear.

Hensley didn't move. Didn't blink. Just watched, letting the silence rot.

"Well?" he said at last, the word floating out, deceptively light.

Morales's voice cracked. "Boss, we... we missed an opportunity."

"There were some cops snooping around, they roughed up a few of our boys." Morales regrouped, swallowing down the panic. "Marco and the fellas took it upon themselves to hire someone, and, well, it didn't pan out."

Silence fell, deep and echoing. Hensley didn't move. Didn't blink. The air in the room grew heavier, pressing against Morales's chest like a weight. Sweat crawled down his spine. His mind spun through every punishment he could imagine, none of them far-fetched.

Then Hensley smiled, thin, clinical. A scalpel's edge. "Is that so?"

Morales blinked, rattled. He'd braced for shouting, threats, anything loud. But this... this quiet was worse.

"Yes, sir," he stammered. "He, uh, got away. I, I'm sorry. But don't worry. I'm calling in the Shroud to take care of it."

Hensley rose, deliberate in every movement, smoothing the front of his tailored suit like a predator readying its strike. He crossed to the window, hands clasped behind his back, staring out at the sprawling city below. City lights fractured in his pupils, cold, reptilian gleams flickering there.

"You're afraid, Morales," Hensley said, voice soft, almost gentle. "Good. Fear keeps you sharp. But this? This is nothing. The Ring doesn't rely on luck, or dead cops. We adapt."

His cufflinks caught the light, tiny silver skulls. Morales had never noticed them before, or maybe never dared to look. He nodded, swallowing hard. His voice cracked. "I, I understand. It won't happen again."

Hensley turned, his gaze suddenly razor-edged, slicing the room in two. "No, it won't. Because if it does, you won't get another chance to apologize."

Morales flinched, pain flaring sharp in his ribs where Hensley's enforcer had cracked them last year. The boss forgave, once. Forcing himself to hold Hensley's eyes, Morales whispered, "We've already made the call."

A tense pause filled the room. Hensley's tone shifted, almost casual, but Morales caught the razor-thin steel beneath it.

"It's time, then. The girls go to the buyers in Macau. The organs? Istanbul. No traces. Unload everything tomorrow night. All of it. The cash, everything. We get out before the heat gets worse."

Morales's breath caught, hesitation thick in his throat. "All of it, sir? Even the-?"

Hensley cut him off with a sharp, precise gesture. "Yes, Morales. All of it. No loose ends. Make the calls. And next time, don't miss. I don't care how many cops stand in your way."

Morales nodded, throat tightening like a noose. "Understood."

He turned to leave, relief and dread warring inside him, but Hensley's voice stopped him, soft, almost gentle, but unmistakably lethal.

"And Morales? Your sister's tuition payments depend on this. Pity if she had to... withdraw. Understood?"

Morales's hand trembled on the doorknob. He nodded, unable to trust his own voice, the crushing weight of the city pressing down as he hurried out. Behind him, Hensley's shadow stretched long and inescapable, the gears of the Ring grinding toward something darker than ever before.

CHAPTER 20: WHY CAN'T WE BE FRIENDS

The three old friends slipped swiftly and silently through the shadows, closing in on a dockside warehouse marked as a likely holding pen for the Ring's victims. Every nerve was on edge, adrenaline thrumming beneath their skin. Colt's mind churned with worry for Beemer; too much time had passed without a word. Today, hopefully, answers would come.

The salt-thick air clung heavy with humidity as Colt crept behind a stack of rusted shipping containers, Bul Armory TAC Pro drawn and ready. The gun was a rare luxury, a retirement gift to himself he rarely trusted. But today, it wasn't sentiment. It was action. Survival.

Colt jerked his chin at Ben, eyes flicking to the pistol as if daring him to measure up. Ben met Colt's gaze, a silent challenge hanging over the surgically tuned tactical weapon, like a son seeking approval from a doting father. His eyes widened at the sight of the firearm, then he smiled and nodded.

Ben breathed in sharply through his nose and pulled out his Sig Flux Legion. With a flick of his finger, he released the spring-loaded brace, which snapped out, transforming the gun from a concealable sidearm into a shoulder-stabilized blaster. He smiled to himself, as if he'd just won something.

For a heartbeat, the two men stood there, weapons gleaming, pride and adrenaline crackling between them.

Mo kept his classic 1911 .45 at low ready, shaking his head at their antics. He'd seen enough gun envy to last a lifetime.

Colt paused to take it in. Just over a month ago, he'd been a ghost, retired, drifting, his toughest choice whether to pour blanco or reposado. Now every decision carried weight, adrenaline surging through his veins. He was back in the field, shoulder to shoulder with the only people he trusted. The stakes weren't just high, they were lethal. After a lifetime forged in fire, how the hell could he hang up his instincts and let them rot in a closet? He couldn't. He wouldn't. Out here, with bullets and betrayal never more than a heartbeat away, Colt felt alive, dangerously alive. This was where he belonged. This was what he was made for.

Before the final approach, Colt keyed his radio. "Shepard One, radio check, all units."

"Shepard Two, loud and clear," Ben replied.

"Shepard Three, lima charlie, right out front," Mo barked.
"Shepard Overwatch, in position, lima charlie," Bear's voice crackled over the comms. Perched high and prone in a hidden spot, he had eyes on everything. His rifle was dialed in, watching every angle.

"Shepard Overwatch here, clean lines on all exits," Bear confirmed.

Mo, methodical as ever, took point, slicing quietly through the gloom toward the warehouse, one of the rumored sites holding the Ring's victims.

His voice came in sharp and clear through Colt's earpiece: "Movement, east side. At the door. Black van. Stay sharp."

Colt's voice was firm over the mic. "Keep it tight, boys. Remember, this is recon only. No engagement." Colt's pulse stayed steady as they closed in on the small building rumoured to hold victims. In the back of his mind, he hoped to find Beemer. He signalled Ben to circle left, slipping between containers thick with brine. The sharp stench of fish guts mixed with something darker, pure evil. Their boots crunched on the gravel as they moved into position. Then the door jerked open. Evan Kane stepped out first, hard-eyed, scanning the shadows. Seven women shuffled behind him, heads down, chained by fear. One stumbled. Evan's snarl ripped through the night. "Keep moving!" He yanked her up and flung her toward the black cargo van idling at the curb. Another thug, thick-necked and mean, brought up the rear. He grabbed the fallen girl by the hair, voice raw and ugly. "Keep up, bitch!"

Ben's finger hovered near his trigger, one breath from changing the math, rage coiling tight in his gut. He keyed his radio, voice tight. "Colt, you seeing this shit? We can't just sit here."

Colt's reply crackled sharp and tense. "This is recon, Ben. We're not ready for assault."

The thug grabbed the fallen girl, barking, "Move it, you worthless trash!" His snarling voice echoed off the crumbling brick.

Barely seventeen, her wrists raw and chafed, the girl stumbled again. Her knees hit the ground; she gasped, breath misting in the cold night air.

"I said get up, you little bitch!" the wiry thug spat, grabbing her arm with iron grip, fingers digging bruises into raw flesh. She whimpered, struggling to find her footing, but he yanked her upright, shoving her hard enough to slam her into the van's cold metal side. Looming over her, his face twisted into a cruel sneer. "You wanna make this harder? Keep it up, and I'll show you what hard really means."

He punctuated the threat with a backhand across her cheek, the sharp crack slicing through the silence.

The other girls shrank back, eyes wide with terror, but kept moving, fear wrapped tight around every neck like a leash.

Ben keyed his radio. "You think these girls care if we're ready? I'm not sitting here watching this shit. Sit back if you want, I'm going in."

Colt cursed under his breath. Ben was already slipping from cover, gun drawn. Colt flanked left, hugging the van's shadow.

"Ben, you take the one in back. I've got the driver," he ordered over the radio, voice low and sharp. Evan shoved the last woman inside and slammed the van doors. Turning toward the driver's side, he never saw Colt coming. Colt barrelled in full-speed, a vertical forearm smashing into Evan's temple. Bone met steel.

Evan's head snapped back, ricocheting off the van with a sickening thud. Colt yanked him by the hair, slamming his skull into the metal again. Three brutal slams, just like he'd drilled into recruits at the academy. Some habits never die. Back then, he'd call it an 'environmental stun' on the Use of Force report. Now, it was just survival. Evan crumpled like dead weight.

Colt spun, yanked open the driver's door. The second thug was climbing in from the passenger side, surprise flickering across his face, gone in an instant as Ben hauled him out by the collar.

Ben's fist, brass knuckles gleaming, crashed into the thug's jaw. The man hit the ground, out cold. "Let's move!" Ben shouted, reaching for the passenger door. Before Colt could respond, the building's door slammed open.

A wild-eyed thug raised a 9mm Sig Sauer MPX. The muzzle flared, automatic fire tore into the van, rounds ripping into metal inches from Ben as he dove for cover.

Colt yelled, "Girls, get down!"

Ben would have been done for, the gunman managed a quick five- or six-round burst before collapsing, Bear's round finding its mark.

High above, Bear racked the bolt on his AI sniper rifle, reloading for a follow-up shot, eyes locked on the kill zone. He didn't need it.

"Nice shot, Bear-Cub," Ben barked into the radio, climbing into the van. "Colt, let's get the hell out of here!"

Colt slid behind the wheel. Tires screamed as they tore away.

Colt tapped his earpiece. "All units, rally point. Now."

Ben crawled into the back, checking their damaged cargo. His hands came away sticky, one girl's wounds already fever-hot beneath his touch, infection setting in.

"Colt, some of these girls are in bad shape. We need to get them to a hospital."

Colt nodded sharply. "Copy that."

He didn't wait for more. The van's tires screamed louder than any radio confirmation as they tore into the night.

"I'm out," Bear keyed, collapsing the bipod on his rifle and sliding backward from his overwatch position.

"Copy," Mo responded. "I'm on those plates. See you at the rally point."

CHAPTER 21: DEATH COMES FOR US ALL

Bear had never truly left the battlefield behind, not in spirit, not in instinct. The military hadn't just trained him; it forged him. Fire-tempered nerves, honed reflexes, a mind wired for split-second decisions, the kind that determined who walked away. But it wasn't the firepower that stuck with him. It was the brotherhood. The bond between men forged in blood and dust, where silence said more than words and loyalty was the only constant in chaos.

Trust had kept him alive. Trust would keep him sharp.

He locked the bolt on his rifle in the shadowed bed of his truck, fingers still tingling from the op, senses razor-wired. The night swallowed the road, but a flicker in the rearview pierced the calm, a bland sedan hugging his six, a little too careful, a little too far back. A ghost tail.

Most wouldn't clock it. But Bear wasn't most people.

"Hmph," he muttered, watching the glint off the driver's sunglasses. "Looks like we've got an admirer."

His thumb hovered, then hit speed dial. "Mo, I've picked up a tail. Black four-door sedan, one occupant. Driver's got shades. Riding the edge of visibility."

Mo's voice crackled back, all edge. "You want backup?"

"Negative. If they're dumb enough to follow me, they're dumb enough to regret it. I'll lose 'em before the fallback."

"Copy. Watch yo' ass, brother."

A grin cut across Bear's face, sharp as the adrenaline now coursing through him. "Always do."

As Bear drove deeper into the night, his world felt changed, but the stakes hadn't. No longer in uniform, he now worked the urban battlefield as a SWAT sniper. The threats were different, hostage takers, cartel enforcers, desperate men with twitchy fingers, but the danger? Just as real.

He wasn't in it for adrenaline or headlines. Never had been.

It was always about the team. The brothers and sisters who rode with him, who trusted his aim when the margin for error was measured in heartbeats.

A flick of the rearview mirror reminded him, he wasn't alone.

The black sedan still lingered. Still trailing.

Bear's lips curled into something between a smirk and a snarl. He tapped the wheel, then veered off the main drag, tires spitting gravel as he cut onto a winding back road slicing through the wild, wooded edge of Hillsborough County.

"Let's see how bad you want this," he muttered, eyes narrowing on the shape behind him.

Loyalty ran deeper in Bear than any oath. He'd buried too many good men, some taken by bullets, others by the quieter war that followed them home. The world moved on. He never did.

Every time he set up his rifle, it was for them. To make it matter.

He would not fail them. Not again. Not ever.

,

Inside the trailing sedan, Silas Stroud watched Bear's every move. His eyes scanned the road, calm, calculating.

A well-worn dossier lay open on the passenger seat, Marcus John Bennett, age 36.

Bear's military ID photo stared back at him. A younger version, still hard-edged. The file was thick, deployment records, commendations, psych evals.

Silas didn't need to look again. He'd memorized every word.

His job wasn't just to follow. It was to understand. To anticipate.

And if the moment came, to act.

The two vehicles pushed deeper into the rural sprawl of Hillsborough County, flat farmland and forgotten roads stretching like scars across the earth.

Bear's eyes stayed sharp on the rearview, but his thoughts drifted, just for a breath, to Beemer.

They'd had a bond. Not the surface-level stuff, but something forged in stillness, long stakeouts, cold coffee, the quiet camaraderie that only came from hours of waiting for something to go wrong.

They came from similar dirt. Knew the silence behind the noise. And when they worked Special Ops together, it was seamless. No need for words.

That's why it stung when she left.

He got it, hell, he respected it. She felt boxed in. The ceiling here was low, and she had a shot to climb. So she took it.

Still, the empty seat beside him hadn't stopped aching.

His hands tightened on the wheel. He could almost hear her laugh again, echoing in the cab like a ghost that wouldn't leave.

I wonder what she thinks about that now, he thought, the question heavier than he expected.

,

Behind him, Silas Stroud kept pace. The black sedan glided like a shadow, patient, calculated.

He checked the speed. Waited.

The moment was nearly right.

Then, without ceremony, he pulled out a sleek phone, thumbed in a code with surgical precision.

A cold smile traced his lips.

"Goodbye, Officer Bennett," he murmured, voice flat and final.

At that moment, hidden beneath Bear's floorboards, a small charge silently ignited. It was subtle, quiet enough that not even the driver felt a thing. But the damage was precise and brutal: the blast severed both the front and rear brake lines in one surgical strike, leaving Bear's truck a speeding coffin with no way to stop.

Under Bear's boots, the brake pedal went dead. He slammed his foot down again, harder. Nothing.

"Shit!" Bear barked, clutching the wheel. "No, no, no, come on!"

The truck hurtled forward, a beast unleashed on blacktop. He yanked at the wheel, muscles straining, but the curve ahead was tight, blind, merciless.

"Hold together, you bastard!" he roared.

The front end clipped a fallen tree, and the world fractured, metal shrieking, glass bursting into razor shards, the truck cartwheeled and barrel rolled, end over end, down the embankment. Then came the silence, ugly, ringing, when it finally slammed to a stop, upside down and bleeding.

Silas watched, expressionless, as the chaos unraveled into silence. He rolled past the wreckage, slow and steady, then stopped a hundred yards out and killed the engine. No witnesses. Just the aftermath.

He stepped out, screwing a suppressor onto his FNX .45 with surgical calm. The woods held their breath, the only sound the soft tick-tick-tick of cooling metal. Silas moved forward, boots crunching through gravel and leaves.

Bear, blood trickling from his temple, coughed, sharp, wet, and spat shards of glass. Through cracked vision, he spotted the lone figure emerging from the road above. "Get up, you son of a bitch," he growled, gritting his teeth as he fought the twisted frame holding him down. He had seconds, maybe less.

His vision swam, but instinct clawed for survival. One hand twitched toward the blade at his hip. Not like this, he rasped, defiance flaring against the flood of pain.

Silas approached the wreckage without hurry, his eyes scanning the tree line one last time for movement. Satisfied, he stepped closer.

Then, with the same calm he'd used to pull the trigger on the brakes, he would lean in and deliver several suppressed .45 slugs into the body of Bear Bennett.

CHAPTER 22: BETRAYAL

Sergeant Dane Sloane was at his wits' end, sweat beading on his brow despite the cool night air. Sloane had done all he could. He had covered for her as long as he could. If he didn't do something now, they would be after him. He would have to answer when it was revealed that she was undercover. The stakes had never been so high. In the past, he dropped some information, looked the other way, he got paid, that was it. A promotion here and there. It was a great arrangement. But then Beemer had to go against the grain. And now he had to do something.

He'd liked Nicole, her stubborn laugh, her refusal to quit. But unless he wanted to end up stuffed in a 55-gallon drum, he didn't have a choice.

He leaned heavily against the hood. His face tightened so tight it ached, and his voice was a razor's edge as he pressed the phone to his ear.

"Yeah, it's me," Sloane muttered, voice low and urgent. "Don't interrupt. Listen up, this is bigger than you think. You've got a rat. Name's Beemer. Undercover. She's deep in your organization right now." He glanced over his shoulder, eyes darting to the rearview mirror, scanning for headlights, for shadows that didn't belong. "You might want to look into it. Fast."

"And there's something else. That guy? The retired cop all over the news? Colt Flynn? They know each other!" His thumb hovered over the 'end call' button, nerves frayed.

A tense silence crackled through the line. On the other end, Tracey Block's breath caught. He stepped out of the smoky back room of Mahuffer's Bar, the Ring's favorite haunt, and pressed himself into the shadows near the bar. His hand was steady as he gripped his own phone, tightening even more.

He walked over to where Jan Morales sat, half-shrouded in shadow, and leaned in close, voice barely above a whisper. "Mr. Morales. We've got a problem. There's an undercover cop in with the girls."

Morales's eyes, cold and sharp as broken glass, snapped to Tracey. He didn't raise his voice, didn't need to. Authority bled from his tone like venom. "Who told you that?"

Tracey swallowed, throat suddenly dry. "Just got the call. Sloane, the cop. He said... her name's Beemer. Nicole Beemer."

Morales's lips curled into a tight, humorless smile. "You sure you heard right?"

Tracey nodded, voice catching. "Positive. They said she's deep. Real deep."

Morales's gaze swept the room like a hawk sizing up prey, every angle, every face. "How long?"

"I don't know," Tracey said quickly. "He didn't give me a ton of information, ya know?"

Morales turned back to him, eyes drilling into Tracey like augers. "Find out who it is. Now. Start with the residential houses. Then hit the warehouses. And Tracey, "

He leaned in an inch closer. "Don't screw this up."

Tracey nodded fast, then motioned to the Ring's enforcers, four men already watching from across the room. They moved as one, piling into a black SUV, tires spitting gravel as they tore off toward the neighborhoods they controlled.

Tracey trailed behind, nerves rattling. He had to find her. Fast.

Meanwhile, back at the warehouse, Beemer moved quietly through the rows of crates and shadows, making her rounds. She was doing the count, the job she'd manipulated her captors into giving her. An inside role. A chance to gather intel without drawing suspicion.

She'd played it so well, so convincingly, that sometimes she had to remind herself who she really was. Undercover. Law enforcement. A cop playing prisoner. But tonight felt different. Heavier. Every creak of the metal beams echoed like a warning. Every shadow felt like it was watching her. The whole warehouse seemed to be holding its breath.

Her hands trembled slightly around her notepad, the pages cluttered with half-heard names, vague numbers, cryptic symbols. The weight of the charade was wearing her down.

She turned a corner, and stopped cold.

There, half-hidden in the gloom, was a girl she knew by memory, not by meeting. A face burned into her brain from hours of case files and police bulletins.

Alena.

Even through the grime, the matted hair, and the bruises, Beemer saw it, those brown eyes. Haunted. Hollow. But alive.

Her breath caught in her throat. Slowly, she stepped forward, her voice barely above a whisper. "Alena? Alena Hernandez?"

The girl flinched, curling back against the wall. Her eyes rose, flickered, and then widened. Shock bloomed. For a flicker of a second, hope fought through the haze, a spark long buried.

"Who... who are you?" Alena rasped, her voice cracked and thin, like it hadn't been used in days.

Beemer knelt slightly, heart pounding, hand reaching out with careful urgency. "My name's Nicole. Nicole Beemer. I'm here to help you."

Her voice wavered but held. "We've been looking for you. You're not alone anymore." Alena's lips parted, but no sound came. Tears welled up, blurring the hollow ache in her eyes. She pressed a trembling hand to her mouth, voice barely a whisper. "I thought... no one was coming. I thought they'd forgotten me."

Beemer knelt beside her, eyes darting nervously over

her shoulder. "I haven't forgotten. We're getting out of here. But you have to trust me, alright? Can you do that?"

Alena nodded, small, desperate, a fragile lifeline thrown in the dark. "Please. Don't leave me. Not again."

A jolt of relief and adrenaline surged through Beemer's veins. "I won't. I promise." She squeezed Alena's hand tight, trying to drown out the pounding in her ears. "Stay quiet. Follow my lead."

This was the moment. Beemer had what she came for, proof, a way out, a chance to pull this whole nightmare apart. But as she glanced around at the silent faces and shadowed corners, the thought crashed in hard: Easier said than done.

Meanwhile, Tracey sat tense in the backseat, enforcers flanking him as the SUV tore toward the warehouses. Ash scrolled through data on his tablet, fingers tapping fast. "Here," he said, pointing at the screen. "An unknown phone pinged the Bravo warehouse two days ago."

Tracey leaned forward, eyes narrowing. "You sure it's not one of ours?"

Ash shook his head sharply. "Nope. This one's on the PD watchlist."

Tracey slammed a fist against the seat. "Son of a bitch! How the hell did she get in?"

Ash shrugged, eyes flat and unreadable.

Tracey straightened, voice cold and sharp as steel. "When we get there, everyone fans out. Check every girl. You hear me? Every single one. She'll stand out somehow."

An hour later, the convoy rolled up to the warehouse. The enforcers spilled out, fanning through the building, barking orders, interrogating women with ruthless efficiency.

Beemer caught the first notes of chaos before she even saw it. Her muscles tensed, heart hammering in her chest. Something was wrong.

Tracey stalked the warehouse floor, Ash at his side. "How's it looking?"

Ash scanned the scattered women. "They're everywhere. We're checking, "

Tracey cut him off sharply. "Well, shit, Ash, find the girl doing the coun, the girl doing the count. Shit, Ash, it's her.

The girl doing the count!"

Ash cursed low under his breath. "Should've fucking known."

Beemer crouched beside Alena, trying to stay calm, when Ash rounded the corner. A voice sliced through the thick tension, loud, mocking: "Nicole Beemer! Undercover Detective Nicole Beemer!"

Beemer froze, cold blood flooding her veins. Tracey's voice echoed down the corridor; eyes locked on her. Ash stood just steps ahead, face unreadable. How did they find her? Did she slip? Leave something behind? Her mind raced, desperate for any escape.

Tracey sneered, closing in like a predator. "Looks like the count came up short tonight. Thought you could play both sides, huh? Gather a little intel, save a damsel or two?"

Beemer forced herself upright, chest rising with forced strength, masking the fear clawing beneath her skin. "I, I don't know what you're talking about."

"Oh, I think you do." Tracey halted inches from her face, eyes glittering with cold menace. "You're sharp. I'll give you that. You got this far." He gave Ash a sharp nod.

Ash stepped forward, a cruel smile twisting his lips as he cracked his knuckles, anticipation heavy in the air.

Without thinking, Beemer shifted, shielding Alena with her body. "Let her go. She's got nothing to do with this,"

Ash's fist collided with her cheek, pain exploding through her skull like a thunderclap.

The world spun wildly, darkness pressing in at the edges of her vision.

Her final thought before blackness swallowed her was the terror in Alena's eyes, and the bitter sting of failure.

And then, nothing.

When Beemer came to, pain was the first thing that greeted her, a relentless, throbbing ache radiating from her nose and cheekbones. She gasped, struggling to breathe through her swollen, blood-clogged nose. Each ragged inhale burned her throat. Blinking hard, she tried to focus, but the world shimmered uncertainly, flickering dim light casting long shadows on the grimy walls.

She sagged against the cold metal chair, wrists bound tight behind her back. Panic clawed at her chest, but she forced her breath steady; no way she would let they see her crack.

A heavy pair of boots came into view. Tracey Block. He crouched down until their faces were level, his eyes sharp, cold, predatory.

Beemer met his gaze head-on, refusing to flinch. "You're making a mistake," she said, voice hoarse but steady. She fought the tremor in her hands, digging her nails deep into her palms. "You don't know what you're doing."

Tracey's lips curled into a cruel, slow smile. "Oh, I think I know exactly what I'm doing, Detective." He leaned in closer, breath hot, sour. "You… should have stayed out of this."

Beemer forced a harsh laugh, more a wheeze. "You're scared. That's why you're rushing. You know they're closing in."

Tracey's eyes narrowed. His hand shot out, slapping her hard across the cheek, pain bursting fresh in her skull. "You still don't get it, do you? It's over for you. I just need to make one call. Someone you know is dying to hear from you."

Ever the fighter, Beemer spat blood onto the floor, glare sharp a blade. "So… who's pulling your strings?"

He straightened, pulling out his phone. "Doesn't matter soon enough."

Beemer's mind raced. She had to stall him, buy herself some time.

"You're not as smart as you think. The police will find me.

They'll find all of you."

Tracey laughed, dialing a number with deliberate slowness.

"Let them come. By the time they get here, you'll be nothing but a memory."

Tracey nodded to Marco as he walked in with two of the Ring's enforcers, followed by Jan Morales.

Ash focused on Beemer and took a few more shots at her face.

Through the haze of the beating, Beemer could barely make out the conversation between the two men.

Morales was speaking with Tracey.

"I'll take this one," he said, motioning toward Alena, who was to her left, in the corner.

"Noooo! You leave her alone!" Beemer struggled to speak through her swollen lip and all the blood.

Glaring at Beemer and accepting the ringing phone from Tracey, Morales said nothing as he put the phone to his ear.

"Colt Flynn?"

Meanwhile, miles away, Dane Sloane gripped the steering wheel of his car, fingers twitching.

The city lights blurred past as he drove, but his mind was stuck in the warehouse, replaying Nicole's last words to him.

"She's stubborn," he muttered to himself. "Should've listened. Should've walked away."

Regret gnawed at him, eating away at the bravado he'd worn like armor. He'd liked Nicole, more than he'd ever admit. But he'd made his choice, thrown in with the wrong side.

Now, he was haunted by the thoughts of what they would do to her.

He slammed his fist against the dashboard, cursing himself.

It was too late to turn back. He'd made his bed. Now he had to live with it.

CHAPTER 23: THE PLAN

Colt met Tim years ago at a Snipercraft seminar in St. Petersburg. His grip was familiar, forged in the Pinellas Suncoast heat and nights of whiskey-fueled trust.

Today, Colt found Tim waiting in the shadowed hallway outside HQ, Tampa's air thick with tension. Tim's eyes were hard.

"We've got a location. The plan's locked in. Briefings in fifteen. Here," He shoved a badge into Colt's hand. "You're in. My team's the best. We'll get her back."

This was it. Tim had stepped up and got the government involved. It was a much better scenario than the four of them going it alone.

As much as he might've felt a little disappointed about not being involved, he knew this was for the best. Besides, he was retired.

Colt clipped the badge to his jacket, heart pounding. He pushed through the door into the briefing room.

The space buzzed with low voices and adrenaline. At the front, a massive screen flickered with grainy surveillance stills; a whiteboard beside it was scrawled with the building's layout, exits, choke points, red Xs marking threats.

Operators lined the walls, armored vests and restless eyes. Tim's team, seasoned, silent, dangerous. Scattered among them, local agency muscle. Medics with trauma kits slung over their shoulders. A negotiator flipping through a battered notepad. Every face was set. Every movement sharp.

Colt took a seat at the rear of the room, scanning the faces. The stakes were high, and the clock was ticking.

There was no room for error, tonight, people's lives hung in the balance.

At the head of the table, the SWAT commander, a grizzled agent with a voice like gravel, clicked a remote. The projector screen flickered to life, displaying the layout of the warehouse, annotated with entry points and the last known positions of the victims and suspects.

They had done their homework. Detailed images of the building from every possible vantage point. Team assignments. Fallback locations. Rally point. Contingency plans, they covered everything.

"We have local civilian SIGINT assets in the area feeding us real-time data along with our own DHS assets," the commander began.

He was referring to Mo. Even though he wasn't currently a government employee, you just didn't ignore skills like his. You used them. Besides, his security clearance outweighed anyone in the room.

"We also have confirmation of at least fifteen victims, and possibly one undercover local agent," the commander continued, nodding toward a plainclothes officer with haunted eyes.

"Victims are being held in the northeast corner, likely restrained. Traffickers are armed, unpredictable, and have a history of violence."

Victims. The risks to the team. And the knowledge that, for some, rescue couldn't come soon enough.

The commander continued, "There was a small, local operation conducted just yesterday where seven victims were rescued, one perp deceased. More on that one later."

The commander eyeballed Colt.

He shifted uneasily, realizing how far outside the lines he'd strayed. Who knows what kind of answers he would have to come up with?

When all this was over, Colt's mind flicked to Ralph, the lawyer who'd always had his back at backyard barbecues.

Not that it would have changed his course of action in any way.

We'll just have to wait and see, he thought to himself.

"Our priority is extraction, get those people out alive. Secondary is apprehension."

Colt's pulse hammered as he scanned the faces of the team.

One of the local agents chimed in, "Some victims are minors. They're terrified, conditioned not to trust uniforms. We need medics and victim specialists ready. Some may bolt or hide when the shooting starts."

The commander nodded. "We have HSI and FBI victim specialists on standby, with interpreters and trauma counselors. Once the site is secure, they'll move in. Remember, traffickers may use victims as shields or bargaining chips. Rules of engagement are clear: protect the innocent at all costs."

A photo of Detective Nicole Beemer flashed on the screen.

"This is a local asset thought to be on the inside. As far as we know, they don't know who she is. Let's keep it that way," barked the commander.

The room fell silent as the gravity of the mission settled over them.

Colt felt the weight of what was at stake, the lives of the victims.

The commander's final words rang out, grim and resolute:

"We move fast, we move hard, and we bring them home. Let's go get our people. Any questions?"

"Run-throughs in five," the assistant team leader barked, voice clipped and hard.

Colt lingered at the edge of the briefing room, adrenaline still humming beneath his skin. Tim's crew were sharp, real operators. They'd get the job done. He told himself that. Tried to believe it.

He stepped out into the hallway, the sterile light flickering overhead. For a moment, he let himself feel relief. He was out. He was supposed to be retired. This was their fight now, not his. He had done what he could.

But as he watched the team gear up, a gnawing restlessness twisted inside him. He wanted in , every muscle in his body screamed for it , but that life was behind him.

Tim intercepted him at the door, helmet in hand, eyes steeled with purpose.

"We'll get her out, Colt. Don't worry."

They clasped hands, a quick, silent exchange of trust forged in darker days.

Tim yanked on his helmet and disappeared with the team, boots pounding out a war drum on the tile.

Colt turned, heading for his truck. The night air was thick with anticipation.

His phone buzzed, a number he didn't recognize.

He answered, voice wary.

"Colt Flynn? Retired Officer Colt Flynn? Is that who I have the honor of speaking to?"

The voice on the other end was smooth, calculating, almost mocking.

Jan Morales. Trouble, wrapped in a name.

"I have someone here you might be interested in speaking with."

Colt's muscles coiled, every nerve screaming, sweat prickling along his brow as he gripped the phone so hard his knuckles clenched.

The silence on the line was a razor's edge.

Then, static, a,

Jagged intake of breath, and Beemer's voice, raw and desperate:

"Colt? Is that you? Listen,"

A scuffle. The phone scraped against something, a muffled curse.

Colt's heart hammered.

A new voice, cold as steel, slid into his ear. Morales.

"Yes, I have her. I know exactly who she is. Don't worry, you'll see her again…"

Colt's stared outwardly.

"If you touch her, "

Morales cut him off, unhurried, almost bored.

"I have your address, Retired Officer Colt Flynn. Don't worry, I'll send her to you…"

A pause. Then Morales's voice dropped to a whisper, venomous.

"I'll return her to you, Colt. Slowly. In ways you'll never forget."

The line went dead.

Colt stared at the phone, breath ragged, his world tilting.

He wanted to scream, to smash something, but his training locked him in place.

He forced himself to breathe. In. Out.

But rage boiled, threatening to shatter his control.

His phone buzzed again, shrill and insistent. He snatched it up.

"Colt, it's Mo. I've been monitoring calls from that warehouse. I got their location. And listen, it's not the one Tim's team is hitting, it's all the way across town."

"Shit!" Colt cursed.

"I'm sending you the location now. I'll have the van set up in twenty," Mo stated matter-of-factly.

Colt was already moving, boots pounding across the floor.

"Get ahold of Ben. Have you heard from Bear?"

"Ben's en route, and Bear's been off grid ever since he picked up that tail," Mo quipped.

"Got it. Keep trying him." Colt's voice was a low growl, urgency slicing through every word.

"Colt, don't do anything stupid," Mo pleaded. "You can't go in there alone. Wait for Ben, at least!"

But Colt was already gone, the call abandoned.

The rear tires of Colt's Silverado smoked as he peeled out of the lot, all 650-horsepower engaged at once.

"Come on, come on," he muttered, hands trembling as he punched the coordinates into his GPS.

Mo's message pinged: a string of numbers, a location that could mean salvation or a trap.

The truck jumped the curb as he tore out of the lot. The world blurred past, streetlights flickering like warning signals. Every second counted. Every mile was a countdown.

His mind raced. What if he was too late? What if Morales made good on that threat? Colt's grip tightened on the wheel. He could still hear Morales's voice, that promise, piece by piece, echoing in his skull.

He pressed harder on the accelerator. The Silverado's engine howled.

"God help Jan Morales," Colt hissed, voice low and dangerous, "or anyone else who stands in my way tonight."

The darkness swallowed him, but Colt didn't care. He was beyond fear, beyond reason.

Tonight, he was riding the darkness, and he wouldn't stop until he got her back or burned everything down trying.

CHAPTER 24: RESCUE OR NOT, HERE I COME

Colt crept through the shadows, every muscle tensed, breath barely stirring the air. He adjusted his LBV, the Velcro whispered as he tightened it across his chest. Each step was measured, deliberate. He paused in the darkness to check his gear: M4 loaded; his thumb flicked the selector switch. 9mm holstered on his thigh, ready. Extra magazines stacked and secure. He exhaled slowly, steadying his breath.

This was reckless. He knew it. Charging in alone was a last resort, but what choice did he have? Every second he hesitated was another second Beemer might not have. Her bloodied face, the desperation in her eyes, haunted him. Ben was en route but still too far out. Bear's radio silence gnawed at him, the last message a warning about a tail, then nothing. Colt's gut twisted with worry.

He pressed his comms button, voice barely above a whisper. "Radio check?"

Static cracked through the comms, then Mo's voice, cool and confident. "Lima-Charlie. I'm your eye in the sky, baby. You're not alone."

Colt managed to smile tightly. "Good. Keep those eyes peeled. I don't like the silence from Bear."

A burst of static, then Ben's voice, rough and distant. "I hear ya, Colt. Still about fifteen mikes out. Don't do anything crazy."

Colt snorted softly. "Define crazy."

Mo cut in, tone sharp. "Drone's up now. Your best point of entry's the small door on the west side. Only one BG posted. Looks bored. You've got a window, but it won't last."

Colt edged closer, crouching low behind a stack of oil drums. The warehouse loomed ahead, its rusted siding slicing the moonlight like a blade. Shadows stretched long across the gravel, silence broken only by the distant hum of traffic. Somewhere inside, Beemer's life slipped away with every passing second.

He scanned the perimeter, eyes narrowed. One sentry paced near the side door, rifle slung carelessly over his shoulder. The man's attention drifted, head on a swivel but not really watching.

Mo's voice crackled in his ear. "Just the one out front. He's got a radio, but he's not paying attention."

Colt drew a deep breath, steadying his nerves. "Copy. Moving." He slipped from cover, his senses pegged at one hundred percent.

Heel-to-toe, weapon raised, M4 just inches below his chin, he could hear his own heartbeat, loud as thunder. He closed the distance, the sentry oblivious until it was too late. Colt squeezed the trigger, two suppressed rounds punched into the man's chest, a third to the head. The body crumpled silently.

He dragged the sentry into the shadows, wiping sweat from his brow. "Sentry down," he whispered. "Moving to entry."

"Thermals show the hallway inside is empty," Mo reported. "You're clear. But be quick, Colt, I'm picking up movement on the east side. Could be nothing. Could be trouble."

Colt pressed his back to the door, took a final breath, and slipped inside. The air was thick with dust and the tang of oil. His boots made no sound on the cracked concrete. He moved fast, slicing the pie at every corner, right foot planted close, as he scanned the oncoming room, ninety percent of the room, then the deep corner. Nothing.

He pressed on, weaving between crates stamped with foreign shipping labels. He could hear the distant clatter of machinery, the faint echo of voices. He kept his weapon up, finger tight just off the trigger.

"Move all the way down that hallway, then through the big door to the left," Mo guided. "I've got eyes on the floor plan."

"Copy," Colt whispered. "Where's Ben?"

"He's moving up to the west side now," Mo replied. "Still clear. Still nothing from Bear."

Colt's responded. "Keep trying. If he's in trouble, I need to know."

He pressed forward, nerves stretched to the breaking point. Suddenly, the wall beside his head exploded in a shower of splinters, gunfire. A shout rang out, boots pounding on concrete. Colt dove behind a forklift, bullets tearing through the air, splintering wood and ricocheting off metal. The stench of gunpowder filled his nostrils.

He peeked around the forklift, spotted a shooter reloading behind a crate. Colt fired, three quick shots, dropping the man. Another muzzle flash from the catwalk above. Colt rolled, glass shattering overhead, shards raining down. He fired upward, the shooter's silhouette jerking before crumpling out of sight.

"Contact!" Colt barked into the comms, voice raw. "Where's my backup?!"

Ben's voice, tense and breathless: "Almost there, Colt! Hold on!"

Mo's voice was urgent now. "Colt, two more moving in from the east corridor! You need to move. Now!"

Colt gritted his teeth. "Copy! Moving!"

He sprinted low, weaving between crates. The warehouse echoed with shouts, he'd lost the element of surprise. Every second counted. He could feel the clock ticking for Beemer.

He pressed his back to a stack of crates, sweat trickling down his neck despite the chill. He heard footsteps, close. Too close. He raised his M4, finger tight on the trigger.

A shadow moved. Colt fired, the report muffled but deadly. Another body hit the ground. He couldn't stop now. Couldn't slow down.

"Mo, talk to me!" Colt hissed. "Where's Beemer?"

A pause, then: "Thermals show several heat signatures in the far office. One's slumped over. That's most likely your target, Colt. But you've got more movement closing in. You need to hurry."

Colt's breath came fast and shallow. "Ben, you better be ready to kick in that door."

Just then, Evan Kane slammed into Colt like a freight train, sending him sprawling. "Remember me?" Evan grinned as Colt went sprawling to the floor, his M4 ripped from his shoulder. Colt remembered. Too bad his "Environmental Stun" wasn't permanent.

On his back, Colt rolled over and immediately went for his secondary weapon, but it was kicked from his hand by Evan.

Colt was crouched, staring at Evan, about thirteen feet away, slowly pulling a Beretta 9mm from his waistband. "You should've stayed gone, Kane."

Evan's eyes locked on Colt, pupils dilated, nostrils flaring, every muscle coiled like a panther about to pounce. Colt's blood pounded through his veins, each beat echoing in his ears like a war drum, but his mind was a razor's edge. He cataloged every detail: the glint of the pistol in Evan's hand, the twitch in his jaw, the way his boots squeaked on the concrete.

Thirteen feet. Not enough distance to run. Not enough to close the gap without eating a bullet. Evan's finger hovered over the trigger. Colt's own pistol wasn't close enough to go for, his only hope was the knife tucked in his vest. He didn't have a gun, but he always had a blade. One of his favorite quotes by SEAL Team 6's first Commander, Richard Marcinko, echoed in his mind: "Knives are like credit cards; don't leave home without 'em, and always carry several."

Most people would freeze in this situation, paralyzed by the primal terror of staring down a gun barrel. Most would beg, or try to reason, or simply shut down. But Colt wasn't most people.

Evan's voice, low and mocking: "You're out of moves, Flynn. This is where you bleed."

Colt's lips curled into a faint, defiant smile as his mind flashed back, years ago, his grandfather's voice echoing in his memory, thick with that indelible Scottish brogue. "Never forget where you come from, lad. Your past is your best teacher. Trust your hands. Trust your eyes."

He remembered Cameron Moore, a mountain of a man, six-foot-three and broad as a barn door, teaching him the art of throwing axes in the Florida sun. "It's all in the wrist, Colton. Let the blade do the work. And remember, sometimes, you only get one shot."

A memory flickered: his grandmother Abigail, arms crossed, watching from the porch. "You're going to put someone's eye out, you two!" Cameron would just laugh, tossing another axe, the sound of his mirth rolling across the yard like thunder.

Colt's grip tightened. He could throw from the blade, let it spin once and a half, or use the no-spin technique, index finger guiding the blade, sending it straight and true. He'd practiced for years, even when Becca came into his life. She'd watched him one afternoon, her eyes bright with mischief. "Axes are barbaric," she'd teased, talking him into throwing knives. "Try something more civilized, cowboy."

Colt had laughed at the irony, there was nothing civilized about hurling sharp steel through the air with deadly precision. She was right, though. Knives were surgical. Knives were personal. Knives left a message.

Evan took a step forward, gun raised.

Colt's voice was ice. "You're not going to shoot me. You're too scared."

The man's face twisted in anger. "You want to bet your life on that?"

Colt's mind raced, calculating the distance, the angle, the man's stance. One last time, he heard his grandfather's voice: "Trust yourself, Colton. Don't hesitate."

The world shrank to a tunnel, just him and the threat.

He shifted his weight, every muscle taut as a coiled spring.

In one fluid motion, Colt hurled the knife. The blade began its rotation, but he stopped it with a flick of his finger, no-spin. Arrow-straight.

It whistled through the air, slicing the silence.

Thwack.

The blade buried deep into Evan's neck. His eyes went wide with shock, gun clattering to the floor as he staggered back, clutching at the wound. Blood spurted between his fingers, hot, dark, alive.

He tried to speak, but only a wet gurgle escaped.

Colt didn't wait.

He exploded forward, a freight train of muscle and fury, slamming into Evan's chest with full force. They crashed to the ground, the impact rattling Colt's teeth. Evan Kane's body convulsed once, then went still.

Colt rolled off, chest heaving, sweat pouring down his face. He stared at the dead man, his knife hand trembling, the moment crashing in like a tidal wave.

This wasn't practice.

This wasn't memory.

This was survival.

He stood over Evan, every nerve alight, heart still jackhammering in his chest. He bent, retrieved his blood-slick blade, and wiped it on his pants with a grimace.

His hands shook, not from fear. From the weight.

Of what he'd done.

Of what it cost.

Another life taken.

Another piece of himself, gone.

He snatched up his rifle and pistol, hands trembling only for a heartbeat before the old, familiar focus snapped into place, cold, precise, automatic.

He pressed his comms, voice raw, urgent. "Mo, Ben, I'm coming up to the back room. Anyone got eyes on?"

The radio crackled, static hissed, then Ben's voice cut through, breathless and tense. "Colt, I just found where they've been keeping the girls. I got my hands full over here, three hostiles down, but more incoming. I need a minute."

Colt muttered a curse, adrenaline flooding like fire through his veins. "Copy that, Ben. Prioritize the girls. Keep your head down."

He was on his own. And he knew it.

He paused at the next door. "Mo, anything on Bear?"

A beat of silence. Then Mo's voice, tight: "Nothing."

Colt's chest tightened. Bear wasn't just a teammate, he was family.

Losing him wasn't an option.

Colt drew a breath, deep and steady. Then moved, boots whisper-quiet on the concrete, weapon up, eyes slicing through the dark.

At the far end of the warehouse, a heavy steel door hung ajar, bleeding harsh fluorescent light into the gloom.

Colt took another breath. Let it anchor him.

Then he kicked the door wide with a crash, rifle ready, heart pounding like a war drum.

He burst inside, gun raised, sweeping the room. A thug by the doorway, Marco, spun, eyes wide. Colt fired first. Rounds tore into the wall as Marco dove for cover.

The air erupted with gunfire, bullets shredding crates and pinging off steel beams.

Ducking in the chaos, Tracey's eyes flicked to the window, already planning his exit. Time to vanish.

Colt returned fire against Marco and two more enforcers. Muzzle flashes strobed at the far end of the warehouse as the pair advanced, sub-guns raised.

Colt sucked in a breath, rolled, and fired twice. One round punched through a rusted drum. The other sparked off a forklift. The enforcers ducked, barking clipped orders, panicked and sharp.

From the shadows, BOOM. Marco's shotgun thundered, the blast chewing a ragged hole in the crate inches from Colt's head.

Colt scrambled, blood pumping, sweat stinging his eyes.

Then, movement. Beemer. Tied to a chair just left of the firefight.

Across the chaos, Tracey made his move. Slipping behind a stack of pallets, he sprinted for the bay window.

Crash!

Glass exploded as he dove through, vanishing into the haze beyond.

Colt popped up. Three sharp shots. One enforcer dropped, hard.

A click, magazine change. Colt's chance.

He surged forward, firing as he moved. His rounds caught the second enforcer in the leg.

The man went down screaming, gun skittering across the concrete.

Marco caught sight of Tracey just as he cleared the window, fleeing into the night.

He shouted, voice cracking with panic, "Tracey! Where the fuck are you going? Get back here, you coward!"

He never finished the sentence.

Colt's aim found him, one seventy-five-grain 5.56 round punched through Marco's forehead. He dropped like a puppet with its strings cut.

Without hesitation, Colt stepped over and delivered a clean safety shot to the head of the enforcer still groaning on the floor.

Then he turned, pivoting fast.

There.

Beemer.

Tied to a battered chair in the far corner, her face streaked with blood, swollen and bruised. Her eyes locked onto Colt's, wide with pain, but burning with hope.

Standing over her was Ash Mercer, lips curled into a cruel smile, a blade pressed tight to her throat.

"One step closer," Ash sneered, voice slick with menace, "and she's done, slow and messy."

Colt froze, lowering his rifle, hands rising slowly. His voice was calm, but glacial. "Easy, buddy. Let her go. You don't want to do this."

Ash's eyes twitched, wild, darting. "Stop moving, cop! One more step, and I swear I'll do it!"

Colt stopped.

Every nerve thrummed, tuned to violence. He measured the distance. The grip. The angle.

Half a second. That's all he'd need.

He feigned a shift. Ash's eyes tracked the motion.

Now.

In a blur, Colt drew his pistol and fired. One clean shot.

The round struck Ash in the temple. His head snapped back, and he crumpled, the knife clattering to the floor.

Silence fell, broken only by Beemer's ragged breath.

Colt rushed to Beemer, hands trembling as he cut her free. "Nikki, you with me? You okay?"

Beemer managed a shaky, bloodied grin. "Took you long enough, cowboy."

He hauled her gently to her feet, adrenaline still pounding through his veins. "We're not done yet. We need to move."

She staggered, clutching her side. "Wait," she gasped, voice raw but urgent. "Alena. We have to get Alena! Morales took her just after they called you. She's the whole reason I'm here, Colt. We can't leave her behind."

Colt saw the fire in her eyes, determined, unwavering. No use arguing.

He keyed his comms. "Ben, Mo, come in. Beemer is secure."

Ben came back, breathless. "That's good news! I'm loading the last of the girls into the RV now. Place is chaos."

Colt's voice was all business. "Mo, can you backtrack, anybody leave right when I got that call?"

"Working on it," Mo replied, voice smooth as ever. "And hey, just got word. Tim's op went down clean. Twenty girls safe."

Ben jumped in. "That's great news."

Mo added, "Bear's comms are back online. Looks like he shook the tail, but I can't pin his location yet."

Colt let out a breath. "Thank God. Keep working it, Mo."

Colt dropped to one knee beside Beemer, his hands trembling as he checked her for hidden wounds.

"What do you say we get out of here?" he asked, voice raw.

"Thought you'd never ask," Beemer said, forcing a breathless grin.

Colt slid an arm beneath her shoulders, careful not to jostle her injuries. She winced, biting back a cry, but didn't protest as he hauled her upright. Her legs buckled, so he half-carried, half-dragged her toward the fractured light spilling through the warehouse's battered exit.

Every step was a battle. Beemer's head lolled against his shoulder, her weight heavy with exhaustion and pain. Colt's boots slipped on shell casings and broken glass, the world tilting with each step. The air stank of gunpowder, sweat, and fear.

At last, they reached the door. Colt kicked it open, rusted hinges screaming, and stepped into the night.

Beemer sagged, knees giving out. Colt tightened his grip, easing her down behind a stack of crates, shielding her from view. He yanked off his jacket and pressed it to the wound at her side, trying to stem the bleeding.

Above, Mo's drone buzzed, circling in wide arcs, scanning for Jan Morales.

Beemer's eyes met his, glassy but defiant. "Wasn't sure you'd make it in time."

Colt gave a grim smile. "You're not that easy to lose."

She tried to laugh, but it came out a rough cough. He squeezed her hand tighter, grounding her as the world spun dizzy and fierce around them, battered but not broken. For now, they had made it out alive, together, and changed forever by the darkness they'd survived.

After a moment of silence, the radio crackled sharply. Mo was back, voice steady. "Colt, I think I found your boy."

Colt barked. "Where is he, Mo?"

"Looks like CCTV caught him about forty-five minutes ago, trying to haul ass outta here, but he must've thought it too hot. He's holed up at the old Holiday Cruise building, on 1st Ave."

Colt got his bearings fast. "Shit, he's right around the corner."

Beemer's eyes blazed with fierce determination. "Then what are we waiting for? Let's go! We can still get that fucker!"

Colt steadied her, eyes sharp, taking in the pain etched deep across her face. She was tough, no doubt, but Ash had done a serious number on her, her breathing was shallow, one eye swollen shut, and blood still trickled from the corner of her mouth.

"Ben, I need you to come pick up Beemer," Colt said into his comm, voice gentle but firm.

Beemer jerked away, anger flaring like wildfire. "No! She's my responsibility. I'm not sitting this out, Colt!"

Colt put a steady hand on her shoulder, calm and reassuring. "Nikki, you're hurt bad. You'd be no help to her like this. Let us handle it. I promise, I'll get her back."

Beemer's eyes filled with frustration and pain, but she nodded, biting her lip hard to keep from crying out.

Ben's voice came through, steady and resolute. "On my way, Colt. Hang tight."

Colt squeezed Beemer's hand, grounding both of them. "You did good, Beemer. Now let us finish this."

He scanned the area quickly, mind already racing through the next steps. Morales was close. The mission wasn't over. Not until every one of them was safe.

CHAPTER 25: THE PRODIGAL SON

His exit route was blocked by the wail of approaching sirens. Without hesitation, Morales quickly hid the vehicle and sought refuge in the old, abandoned fish processing building, a sparse, cavernous place with plenty of room to disappear. Jan Morales dragged Alena roughly by the collar out of his black BMW as she fought against him. "Keep moving!" he snarled.

As Colt closed in, he barked into his comm, "Talk to me, Mo! You got anything?" Mo's voice crackled back, "Looks like he just dipped into the old fishery, two clicks from your location. He's got the girl."

Colt ran on pure adrenaline now. His ribs, already broken, screamed in protest, and jagged lacerations from bullet fragments burned fresh across his skin.

Drawing closer, he spotted the black BMW haphazardly parked, its passenger door wide open. He moved cautiously, slipping between stacks of rotting pallets and rusted machinery.

Mo delivered a cautionary message over the radio, "Colt, drone battery is dead, heading back to base. You should wait for Ben."

"Roger that," Colt let out an exhausted sigh. "This needs to end now," he said aloud, steadying himself, then moved in.

Morales dragged Alena, one arm locked tight around her throat, the other clutching a pistol like it weighed a ton.

Colt approached cautiously, staying low and weaving through the maze of crates for cover. Constantly scanning every angle, he did his best to cover every possible avenue of attack. He reached the rear of the building, near the loading docks and sea access.

That's when he saw Alena, tied to a chair, her head slumped near an old dumpster. Morales was nowhere in sight. It didn't look good. This was the perfect setup for an ambush. She was completely exposed. The spot had boat dock access as well as truck access, leaving it wide open all the way to the roadway.

Colt froze, every nerve on edge. Alena wasn't moving. He couldn't afford hesitation. Morales was baiting him, and Colt knew it.

He thumbed his mic, voice low and urgent. "Mo, do you copy? Anyone on comms?" Static spat back at him, a garbled hiss. Someone was out there, trying to reach him, but the signal was shredded, distance or deliberate jamming, he couldn't tell. Colt's gut twisted. Charging in blind would get him killed and leave everyone else screwed. He forced himself to wait, every instinct screaming for action.

Colt swept the refinery with his LPVO, glassing every shadow. "Where are you, Morales? I know you're out there," he muttered, eyes slicing through the gloom.

A sniper's patience was a weapon. Colt wielded it, holding his breath, counting heartbeats. Then, a scuffle behind him. Movement. At the far end of the refinery, behind a barricade of warped pallets, Beemer emerged, pistol raised, eyes locked on Alena. She was going to break cover to try to save her.

Colt clenched his jaw and cursed, "Dammit, Nicole! I told you to stay put!"

He tried to signal her, but any move would blow his position. Helpless, he watched as Beemer crept toward Alena, knelt, and set her weapon down, hands moving to untie the bindings.

The shot cracked like thunder. Beemer jerked, clutching her chest, and collapsed behind Alena.

Colt's blood iced over. He swept the area, desperate to spot the shooter. Beemer writhed on the ground. Another shot, this one from behind a heap of rusted canning equipment. Colt zeroed in, adrenaline spiking. He exploded from cover, sprinting out from behind a forklift, closing on the debris where Morales had to be.

He rounded the pile, rifle up. The shot came fast, a white-hot punch to his side as Jan's bullet tore through the edge of his vest, glancing off the ballistic plate. Colt crashed down, blood soaking his shirt. From the ground, he saw Jan stalking forward, gun drawn, a predator closing in for the kill.

Another crackling key-up came from the radio, but still, nothing was audible.

Colt fought to breathe, to focus. He struggled to draw his pistol and bring it up on target, but by the time he managed, Morales was there, pinning his arm beneath his boot. Colt's vision blurred, not just from blood, but from the crushing weight of failure, Alena, Beemer, all of them counting on him.

"You know, Flynn, I used to believe there was a line between monsters and men. That if I just kept my head down, did my job, I'd stay on the right side of it." He let out a bitter laugh, his finger tightening on the trigger. "Turns out, the line moves. Every time you think you've found it, you look down, and your boots are already on the wrong side.

Colt tried to push himself up, but his strength failed. Morales shoved his boot harder into Colt's hand. "I'm not looking for forgiveness. Not from you, not from anyone. But I want you to understand, every choice, everybody, it all adds up. And in the end, the weight's too much for any man to carry."

He took a breath, gun aimed square at Colt's head. "You're not the hero you think you are. Neither of us is. We're just the last men standing in a room full of ghosts."

Colt's mind raced, chest pounding. Did he have any options? What could he do? His choices were quickly narrowing as Morales raised his pistol one last time, pointing it straight at Colt's head.

Just then, a crackling came over the radio. Colt couldn't make it out at first, but then another unmistakable key-up.

Then, in a brutal spectacle, Morales's head erupted in a crimson haze, a striking spray of fine red mist, shattered bone, and fragments of brain matter painting the air in chaos. The destruction came courtesy of a .308 caliber bullet, tearing through his skull at a blistering 1,600 feet per second. The round had entered the rear of his head after carving a deadly path through the packing yard, from over the parking lot and through the maze of heavy machinery on the north side of the complex.

The shot came from a sniper position buried at the far end of the complex, right at the edge of the compound, three hundred and forty-six yards away from the target, an almost invisible vantage point. From there, the bullet originated at the muzzle of an Accuracy International AXSR Sniper Rifle, traveling at 2,700 feet per second with surgical precision.

Behind the rifle stood Bear Bennett, Colt's protégé, still bloodied and beaten from his encounter with the Shroud. Despite the pain, Bear adjusted his scope, blood dripping down his face, forcing him to wipe it away before the shot so he could see. He breathed steadily and pressed the trigger, sending the projectile that saved his mentor's life.

Bear had crawled into his position just minutes before taking the shot. He could hear the radio traffic from Colt but was unable to transmit.

Just hours earlier, Bear's world had gone sideways, literally. Blood streamed down his face as he hacked up shards of glass, the sharp taste of metal lingering in his mouth. His truck had careened off the road, brakes dead, skidding out of control. He fought the wheel, muscles screaming, barely keeping the wreck from flipping end over end. Through the spiderwebbed windshield, a lone figure emerged on the asphalt, closing in.

"Get up, you son of a bitch," Bear snarled, voice raw. His hands fumbled for his Microtech SOCOM Elite pocketknife. The seatbelt felt like a noose. He slashed it, the blade biting through fabric, then shoved himself toward the passenger window. Every breath stabbed into his ribs. Sweat trickled into his eyes, blurring his vision.

No time. He dropped out of the window, landing in a deep, cold, mud-filled bog. He was immediately submerged and took advantage of the situation and his training, ignoring the numbing pain from his broken ribs, maybe worse. He forced himself to move slowly underneath the half-submerged truck, making himself completely invisible to anyone around him. Sliding under the water, he then low-crawled away from the twisted wreckage, desperate to put distance between himself and the unknown enemy who wanted him dead.

On the road, Silas Stroud stalked toward the ruined truck. He scanned the empty stretch, every sense sharpened. Once sure he was alone, he peered inside, silencer ready. The plan was simple: put a few .45 slugs into Bear Bennett's skull, confirm the kill, and disappear.

But Bear was gone.

Silas's eyes narrowed. He swept the tree line, calculating. The woods pressed close; shadows thick. Could Bear have made it that far, wounded? Maybe. The bastard was ex-military, a sniper. This terrain was his element.

Silas hesitated, then turned away. No sense risking an ambush. The Shroud never played a losing hand. He'd come back for confirmation. For now, Bear was a ghost, and the hunt had just begun.

As he walked calmly back to his car, Silas tapped a number into a small burner phone. "Bennett's down, but Flynn's still a problem. Yeah, he wanted them both gone." He closed the phone, gave one quick look back, and quietly drove off.

Back behind the gun, Bear racked his bolt to the rear, then chambered a follow-up round. "Shot away," he keyed up over the radio, he didn't need the follow-up. The first one ended Morales's reign in an instant.

After Jan's body dropped, Colt got up and staggered over to Beemer and Alena. Beemer's gunshot was only a flesh wound in the arm, and the second gunshot had apparently missed. "Thought I told you to stay put, girlfriend," Colt said, annoyed. "Yeah, well, if you remember correctly, I never really listened to you before," Beemer coughed.

Beemer untied Alena's ropes as Colt dropped on his butt, holding his side. He was badly injured. Alena's pulse was faint, but her hope was strong. "You're okay now, Alena. We got you. It's over."

CHAPTER 26: TAIL BETWEEN YOUR LEGS

Tracey Block sprinted through the broken shadows of the alley, lungs burning, blood pounding in his ears louder than the gunfire he'd just escaped. Each step sent a jolt of pain through his legs, but he didn't dare slow down. His hands shook as he wiped sweat from his brow, the metallic tang of fear sharp on his tongue. Morales had promised him a cut, a future. Now it was all ashes, scattered by muzzle flashes and the screams still echoing behind his eyes. He was just another loose end, and he knew what happened to loose ends.

He darted behind a dumpster, pressing himself flat against the rusted metal, chest heaving. He kept glancing over his shoulder, half-expecting to see Marco's ghost loping after him, eyes hollow, lips twisted in accusation. "You said you had my back, Tracey," Marco's memory seemed to whisper, voice thin and cold. Marco, who'd trusted him. Marco, who'd gone down in the crossfire, and whose death Tracey couldn't shake. Maybe it was guilt, maybe paranoia, but every shadow seemed to flicker with Marco's curse, every echo a whispered threat.

"Not now, Marco," Tracey hissed under his breath, trying to shake the image. "You're dead. I'm not. That's the difference."

He'd left the others behind, no sense dying for a boss who'd already written him off. Survival was all that mattered now. Live to fight another day, he thought, but the words felt hollow. All he needed was a way out, a car, a shadow to melt into before the blue lights caught up.

Then he saw it. A battered black van caught his eye, parked at the edge of the lot, silent, engine off, windows dark with grime. A communications van, he guessed. Probably some tech geek inside, too busy fiddling with radios to notice death creeping up on him.

Tracey grinned, adrenaline sharpening his senses to a razor's edge. He slipped a knife from his belt, hugging the wall, every muscle coiled tight. "Easy kill," he muttered, voice barely more than a rasp. "Take the van, dump the body, and I'm halfway to the interstate before anyone knows I'm gone."

He crept closer, boots crunching on shattered glass. He could see the van's side door slid open just a crack, spilling a sliver of blue light onto the pavement. Inside, he could imagine the faint clatter of a keyboard, the static buzz of a police scanner. Someone was talking, nervous, high-pitched, oblivious. Was he in for a surprise?

Mo had been running on fumes, pushing through nearly twenty-four hours without a break. His eyes burned with exhaustion, but there was no time to slow down. Since he held a top-tier security clearance, the usual hassle of asking Tim for an access badge was a thing of the past. In fact, the guards practically handed it to him without a second glance.

"You're looking rough, Mo," Tim said over the comms, his voice crackling with static but laced with concern. "You sure you can keep this up?"

Mo cracked a tired smile, rubbing the back of his neck. "No choice, Tim. But we're wrapping it up now."

Having worked as a private contractor for DHS and various government agencies, Mo was no stranger to high-stakes operations. His clearance granted him access to an arsenal of tools and tech most could only dream of. "I'm juggling two ops at once," Mo muttered, eyes flicking to the screens in front of him. "Helping you across town while keeping comms tight with Colt and the crew."

"You're a one-man army," Tim chuckled, but the tension in his voice betrayed the pressure they were under.

A red light blinked on the console. Mo's heart rate kicked up. "Hold on, I've got movement." Mo stopped, eyes squinting. "Hmmm, what do we have here?"

Tim's voice sharpened. "Movement? Where?"

Mo's hands glided over the keyboard. "Just outside my van. Stand by, Tim. I'll get back to you."

When DHS kicked off their sweep, Mo didn't hesitate. He shifted his position, moving closer to Beemer's location to centralize his efforts and maintain better control.

Now he was just playing cleanup. The weight of the operation started to lift. But it seemed he had one last rat to kick out of the nest.

Mo watched Tracey's approach on a bank of screens, fingers hovering over mismatched switches. He'd seen Tracey's type before, putting on a good show but no patience for details. Mo's lips curled into a tight smile as he gnawed a black Twizzler, Miles Davis whispering cool jazz in the background.

Mo flicked a switch to unlatch a hidden panel beneath the dashboard. He leaned forward, eyes narrowing. "Let's see how you feel about a little charge."

Outside, Tracey moved like a shadow with a grudge. He wasn't the strongest, but he was fast, and tonight, that had to be enough. He skirted the pools of light cast by the streetlamps, blending into the darkness. He thought he was invisible.

Tracey pressed his back to the van, heart pounding. He could almost feel Marco's presence behind him, icy fingers at his neck. "You're really gonna do this, Trace?" he imagined Marco saying. "After everything?"

"Shut up," Tracey whispered. "I do what I have to."

He peered through the grimy window. He couldn't see inside, he thought to himself, this guy has no idea how close to death he is.

Tracey tightened his grip on the knife. "Sorry, pal," he breathed. "Wrong place, wrong time."

He reached for the door handle, every nerve on fire. Sirens wailed in the distance, growing louder. Tracey's pulse spiked. He had seconds, maybe less. The van was his ticket out, but every instinct screamed nothing was ever this easy, not for him.

He hesitated, just for a heartbeat, as the memory of Marco's last look flashed before his eyes. Then he yanked the door open, knife raised, and the night exploded into chaos.

Tracey grabbed the sliding door handle, ready to ease it open silently and take out the clueless inhabitant. But that didn't happen. The moment he touched the handle, an electrical charge surged through him. Mo had activated a live circuit, sending a continuous current through Tracey's body. He couldn't let go, he was frozen.

A massive jolt of electricity shot through him, white-hot and merciless. Tracey's body locked, muscles seizing, knife clattering to the ground. He couldn't let go. He couldn't scream. Agony roared through his nerves, sweat stinging his eyes, pouring down his face as his body convulsed.

Frozen, Tracey clung to the door handle, powerless to move. Then, slowly, the door slid open from the inside, and he came face-to-face with a sawed-off, double-barreled twelve-gauge. Mo stood there, a half-eaten Twizzler dangling from his lips. "Picked the wrong van, I think."

Tracey's eyes went wide with terror.

From a distance, the sharp report of double buckshot from a short-barreled weapon cracked through the night.

People underestimated Mo. They only made that mistake once.

CHAPTER 27: NO GOOD DEED

A light after-rain drizzle began to fall onto the shattered warehouse roof as red and blue lights began to litter the site. Colt tried to get to his feet as Ben arrived in the RV. Ben would have made a top-notch first responder, he immediately triaged the three and went to work on the one in most immediate need, which happened to be Colt. He had an open pneumothorax, or what is more commonly referred to as a sucking chest wound. Ben cut off his plate carrier and placed an occlusive dressing over the wound.

Meanwhile, Beemer self-administered a tourniquet and began to check on Alena. Alena was groggy and dehydrated but mostly okay.

As Colt lay there, he was able to take in the entire scene. Sirens wailed in the distance, echoing off the twisted metal of the building where, moments ago, chaos had reigned.

Beemer, focused, clung to the trembling shoulders of Alena Hernandez, her face streaked with grime and terror, huddled beneath Colt's battered jacket.

Colt's chest heaved, each breath sharp and ragged, as if his lungs scraped against broken glass. The acrid taste of gunpowder clung to the back of his throat, refusing to let go. Around him, chaos reigned, the aftermath of a rescue operation that had torn through three counties like wildfire. He'd done what he had to do. He'd saved lives. But the cost was everywhere: bullet-riddled walls, shattered windows, and the ruined remains of someone's illicit empire bleeding into the night.

Paramedics arrived and took over for Ben, kneeling beside Colt, hands quick and efficient as they wrapped gauze around his torso. "Hold still, sir," one murmured, voice steady despite the tremor in her hands. "You're lucky. This could've been a lot worse."

Colt managed a grim smile, wincing as the bandage tightened.

"Define lucky," he rasped, glancing down at the blood staining his shirt. "I feel like I just went three rounds with a freight train."

She shot him a look, half amusement, half concern. "You're still talking. That's a good sign." Another paramedic hovered nearby, prepping the gurney. "We're going to get you out of here, okay? Just hang on."

Colt's gaze flicked across the scene. Uniformed officers moved through the carnage, voices clipped and urgent as they took statements from the other shivering victims. One survivor, a woman with a split lip and haunted eyes, caught his gaze. She mouthed, "Thank you." Colt nodded, swallowing hard against the lump in his throat.

Crime scene techs snapped photos, their cameras flashing in the darkness. One of them, a young guy buzzing with nervous energy, paused beside Colt. "You the one who went in first?" he asked, awe mingling with disbelief.

Colt forced a shrug, trying to ignore the pain radiating from his ribs. "Didn't have much choice. Someone had to."

The tech shook his head, glancing at the bullet holes peppering the drywall. "Hell of a thing. You ever get used to this?"

Colt's eyes hardened, memories flickering behind them. "You don't get used to it. You just get better at surviving."

A detective strode over, voice low and urgent. "We need your statement, Colt. As soon as the medics clear you."

Colt nodded. "I'll give you what I can. But you're not going to like what you hear."

The detective's lips thinned. "After tonight, I don't think anything's going to surprise me."

As the paramedics lifted him onto the gurney, Colt's vision blurred at the edges. Sirens wailed in the distance, mingling with the crackle of radios and the low murmur of survivors. He closed his eyes, the weight of what he'd done, and what was still to come, settling heavy on his chest. The battle was over, but the war was far from won.

Colt watched the chaotic aftermath unfold as they loaded him into the ambulance. He locked eyes with Beemer one last time. In that brief, silent moment, gratitude and grief warred on his friend's face. Beemer knew exactly what he had risked and sacrificed. His family. His friends. His safety. His peace. His life. And she would never forget it.

Later, under the harsh fluorescent lights of the hospital, Colt lay half-upright in a bed, trying to come down from the adrenaline spike earlier. The corridor outside buzzed with tension, Beemer, Ben, Mo, and Bear clustered together, voices low and sharp-edged.

Ben glanced at the clock. "They're late. That's not good."

Mo's eyes darted toward the elevators. "Something's coming. I can feel it."

Bear grunted, "Let 'em come. After tonight, I'm ready for anything."

The elevator doors slid open with a metallic groan. An entourage of police detectives strode out, badges flashing, Chief Randall Hayes leading the pack, broad-shouldered, smug, his presence thickening the air. The group moved with purpose, boots echoing like a warning.

Beemer stepped forward, arms outstretched. "Hey, what's going on here? Colt's barely conscious, "

Hayes didn't even glance at her. The detectives brushed past, a wall of blue and gray, storming into Colt's room.

Kowalski, the stone-faced detective from the State Attorney's task force, avoided Beemer's glare as he read from a warrant. "Colt Flynn, you are under arrest for multiple counts of homicide, destruction of private property, and endangering public safety."

Colt's mind raced. He let out a bitter laugh, voice hoarse. "You're kidding, right? I just saved half this city."

Another detective snapped a cuff onto Colt's left wrist, chaining him to the hospital bed. The click of metal was final, cold. "You think I'm going anywhere?" Colt growled.

Colt stared at the cuffs, the cold metal a stark reminder: heroes didn't always walk free.

Beemer shoved her way in, eyes blazing. "Kowalski, are you out of your mind? He saved us all, he saved you! How can you do this? Can't you see the big picture?"

Kowalski looked at her. "I know, Beemer. I know. But the State Attorney called me directly. They want someone's head for this mess."

Beemer's voice cracked with fury. "Someone's head? You want a head? There's one splattered all over the courtyard, go collect that!"

Suddenly, Chief Hayes's voice boomed, filling the room with threat. "I'd watch my step if I were you, missy! You're lucky you're not in cuffs yourself. And as for your career, don't think I won't have something to say about that."

The hallway erupted in commotion. Tim appeared with two federal agents, all business, eyes scanning for threats. He shook hands with Ben and Bear, then strode into Colt's room, his voice slicing through the tension. "Chief Hayes?"

Hayes spun, bristling. "Who the hell are you?"

Tim's badge flashed. "Federal Agent. We need to talk, now." Before Hayes could react, the two agents closed in.

"Let's talk about careers, shall we?" Tim said commandingly.

"What's the meaning of this?! I'm the goddamn Chief of Police!" spat Hayes.

"Not for long, I think," Tim responded. "Your badge won't protect you now. We've got everything. Randall Hayes, you are hereby charged with Obstruction of Justice, Racketeering, Conspiracy to Commit Sex Trafficking, Fraud, and Coercion. Now, let's see about those cuffs."

He nodded to the two agents, and they slapped the former Chief into handcuffs.

Colt watched the drama from his hospital bed. He nodded to Tim with a small smile. "Nicely done."

As they hauled Hayes away, Beemer leaned down to Colt, whispering so no one could hear, "You're not the villain here, Colt. I'll make them see that."

Ralph Marchetti might not have been the gun-toting tactician like Colt and Tim, but he was damn good at poker, a skill that, in Colt's mind, required just as much nerve. Colt still remembered the first time they met, more than twenty years ago, when the moving truck rumbled up next door and Ralph, sleeves rolled up, wiped sweat from his brow and grinned. Their kids, wild with the energy of summer, had become fast friends, darting between yards while the adults exchanged cautious nods over the fence.

Back then, Ralph had seemed like just another neighbor, but it didn't take long for Colt to realize there was more to him. "You ever play Texas Hold'em?" Ralph had asked one evening, flipping a deck of cards between his fingers with practiced ease. Colt shrugged, feigning indifference. "A few hands. You any good?" Ralph's answering smile was sly. "I hold my own.

Maybe you'll get lucky."

From that night on, their friendship was forged over backyard barbecues thick with the scent of hickory smoke and the low burn of bourbon. The two men would lounge in battered lawn chairs, the glow of cigars illuminating their faces as dusk settled in. "You know, Colt," Ralph would say, exhaling a plume of smoke, "the law isn't all that different from poker. It's about reading people, knowing when to hold back, when to push." Colt would laugh, but he listened. He always listened. Their conversations often drifted into legal territory, Ralph dissecting court cases with the precision of a surgeon. "You see, the prosecution overplayed their hand here," he'd say, tapping ash into a tray. "If they'd waited just a little longer, the defense wouldn't have seen it coming." Colt admired the way Ralph's mind worked, sharp, methodical, always three moves ahead. But despite Ralph's reputation as a top-notch attorney, Colt had never asked for legal help. It was an unspoken rule between them, a line neither wanted to cross.

Tonight, though, the air was different, charged, uneasy. Colt's phone call was one out of necessity. He hesitated, the silence over the phone stretching between them like a live wire. "I need your help, Ralph. Not as a neighbor. As an attorney."

Ralph's poker face slipped just for a second. "Well, damn, Colt! It's about time. Cheryl and I have been watching the news for a week, worried sick about you, wondering when you were gonna call."

Colt nodded, the weight of the moment settling on his shoulders. "I know. I'm sorry I didn't call sooner. I didn't have a choice."

For the first time in twenty years, the rules had changed. And as the night deepened, Colt realized just how much he was about to gamble.

Ralph's voice was steady, as always. "Don't talk, Colt. I know the DA. I'll be on the phone with her directly tomorrow morning, stay quiet. You saved lives, I'll make sure they know it."

CHAPTER 28: SOMETIMES JUSTICE ISN'T BLIND

The marble corridors of the Pinellas County Courthouse echoed with the heavy tread of Colt Flynn's boots. A storm brewing behind his eyes. Overhead fluorescents cast harsh shadows on the faces of the press crowding the hallway, their cameras flashing like lightning. Colt ignored them, focusing on the double doors ahead, Courtroom 3B, where his fate would be decided.

Inside, the air was thick with tension. The state prosecutor, a woman known for bloodthirsty indictments, shuffled her papers with deliberate calm. The judge, a stern figure with a reputation for zero tolerance, glanced over his glasses at Colt, then at the defense table.

Bear and Beemer sat rigid in the back row of the courtroom, uniforms immaculate, faces carved from stone. Beside them, Ben, Mo, Tim, and Alena Hernandez formed a silent wall of support. Alena, still pale and visibly shaken, caught Colt's eye. She straightened, chin up, and gave him a small, grateful nod, a silent thank you that cut through the tension like a blade.

Colt felt the weight of every stare in the gallery. The air was thick with whispers, the scrape of shoes, and the nervous flutter of hands wringing programs. Somewhere, a reporter's pen scratched furiously. The judge's bench loomed above, wood polished to a cold sheen, and the American flag hung limp in the stale air.

Ralph Marchetti, Colt's lawyer and oldest friend, leaned in close. His suit was razor-sharp, silver cufflinks glinting under the harsh lights, his expression unreadable. "Keep your cool, Colt," he murmured, voice barely above a whisper. "Let me handle this. No matter what they throw, don't react."

Colt nodded, his fingers flexing beneath the table. His mind replayed the chaos, the warehouse firefight, the desperate chase through rain-slick streets, the split-second decision to save his friends instead of running. He'd do it again. Every second burned behind his eyes.

He glanced at Alena. Her haunted gaze met his, and he remembered the terror in her eyes when he'd pulled her from the wreckage. He'd risked everything for her. Would that matter now?

The prosecutor, a sharp-featured woman in a severe navy suit, stood abruptly. Her voice rang out, slicing through the murmurs. "Your Honor, the state seeks to indict Mr. Flynn on multiple counts: reckless endangerment, obstruction of justice, and unlawful possession of a firearm. His actions, though dramatic, placed civilians at unacceptable risk."

A ripple of unease spread through the gallery. Beemer's fists tightened in her lap. Ben leaned forward, lips pressed into a thin line.

Ralph rose slowly, every movement deliberate. He buttoned his jacket, smoothed the lapels, and faced the judge. "Your Honor let's call this what it was, a massacre in the making. Mr. Flynn intervened when law enforcement was outgunned and outmaneuvered. He risked his life to save others. The so-called 'reckless endangerment' was, in fact, heroism."

The judge rapped his gavel, eyes narrowing. "This is not a forum for grandstanding, Mr. Marchetti."

Ralph's smile was thin, dangerous. "Then let's talk facts. Every survivor in this room owes their life to my client." He swept a hand toward Alena, Bear, and Beemer. "The state's own witnesses credit Mr. Flynn with their rescue. The authorities failed to respond in time. My client acted when no one else could. And let's not forget, thanks to Mr. Flynn's evidence, the real criminals, like former Chief Hayes, are finally facing justice.

The prosecutor bristled, voice rising. "Hero or not, Mr. Flynn broke the law. He endangered lives in the process, "

Ralph cut her off, voice like steel. "But it does mitigate. And as we've already discussed with the District Attorney's office, my client is prepared to offer full cooperation. He will testify, provide evidence, and help clean up the mess the real criminals left behind. In exchange, we seek dismissal of all charges."

A tense silence fell. The judge's gaze flickered between Colt and the prosecutor; pen poised over the docket. The prosecutor hesitated, then gave a reluctant nod.

The judge's voice was grave. "Very well. Mr. Flynn, you will not be charged, provided you cooperate fully with the ongoing investigation. Court is adjourned."

The gavel struck, the sound echoing like a gunshot. Colt let out a breath he hadn't realized he was holding, shoulders sagging as the weight of the world eased, just a fraction.

Ralph clapped him on the shoulder, voice low and urgent. "Let's get out of here before they change their minds."

As they filed out, the press surged forward, cameras flashing, voices shouting questions. Ben and Mo flanked Colt, forming a protective barrier. Beemer squeezed Colt's arm, her uniform crisp, eyes soft with relief. "We've got your back, always, Flynn. Don't forget it."

Colt glanced at Ralph as they pushed through the crowd. "Ralph, I owe you more than I can ever repay."

Ralph grinned, eyes glinting with mischief and relief. "We've been through worse, Colt. You'd do the same for me. Now, let's get a drink before someone changes their mind."

Outside, the sky was bruised with the promise of rain. Colt looked back at the courthouse, the judge's words still ringing in his ears. For now, at least, he was free, but the war wasn't over. Not by a long shot.

CHAPTER 29: LOOSE ENDS

Sergeant Dane Sloane kept his ear pressed to the police radio, the static-laced voices barely audible over the relentless drum of rain hammering the precinct roof. The city outside throbbed with distant sirens and the ceaseless hum of midnight traffic, a living thing just out of reach. Inside, harsh fluorescent lights flickered overhead, casting long shadows across the bullpen. Sloane sat rigid behind his battered desk, his eyes snapping to the glass doors every few seconds. The walls felt like they were closing in, inch by inch. He'd always believed he had friends in the right places, until today, when the phone calls stopped and the favors dried up.

He gripped his chipped coffee mug hard, the bitter taste of burnt coffee mingling with the memory of Beemer's bloodied face, eyes wide with betrayal. Sloane had told himself it was just business, a necessary evil. But the lie curdled in his gut now, sour and unshakable.

A sudden crash shattered the uneasy quiet, the double doors slammed open, banging against the walls. Every head in the room snapped up. Internal Affairs Lieutenant Dominic Reyes strode in, expression carved from granite, flanked by two uniformed officers and a pair of detectives from Organized Crime. The detectives' faces were hard, unreadable, their locked on Sloane. The bullpen froze, a collective breath held. Even the rain seemed to pause, as if the city itself were listening.

Reyes's voice cut through the tension, cold, sharp. "Sergeant Sloane, stand up. Hands where I can see them."

Sloane's chair screeched across the linoleum as he shoved it back, heart pounding so loudly he barely heard his own voice. "What the hell is this, Reyes? You want to tell me what's going on?"

Detective Moore stepped forward, a thick case file clutched in his hand. He dropped it onto Sloane's desk with a heavy slap, papers spilling out, photos, transcripts, evidence bags.

"We know you fed intel to Morales's crew," Moore said, voice low and steady. "We know you set up Beemer. And we know you nearly got her killed because of it. For what? A few dirty dollars?"

A ripple of shock and outrage swept through the bullpen like a lightning strike. Someone muttered, "No way," while another cop's fist clenched tightly around a pen, the plastic creaking under the strain. Sloane's face twisted, defiant for a heartbeat, but the fight drained from his eyes the moment a uniform stepped behind him, cuffs at the ready and judgment already passed.

"You're making a mistake," Sloane spat, his voice trembling with desperation. "You think I wanted this? You think I had a choice?"

Reyes leaned in, close enough for Sloane to feel the heat behind his whisper, words honed like a blade. "You sold out Beemer for a payout, Dane. That's not a cop, that's a coward. You put one of our own in the ground for a payday."

Sloane's lips quivered. His shoulders sagged, as if the weight of the truth had finally landed. "You don't understand, Reyes. They had me, Morales's guys, they had me cornered. They threatened my family. What was I supposed to do?"

Moore slammed a photo onto the desk, loud enough to make heads turn, a grainy shot of Sloane meeting with a known Morales enforcer. "Save it for your lawyer," he growled. "We've got a cell phone recording, Sloane. Your voice, clear as day, found on Tracey Block's body. Block was always looking for leverage, and he got it, right before someone put two barrels of buckshot in his chest."

PREVIOUSLY:

Mo slowly stepped off the platform of the van onto the concrete, careful not to step into the dark, spreading pool of Tracey's remains. The echo of the shotgun blast still rang in his ears, fading into a hush broken only by the ragged thunder of his own breath and the sharp, metallic tang of cordite hanging in the air.

Tracey's body lay sprawled on the ground, chest a ruin of red and bone, the double-barreled shotgun still smoking faintly in Mo's grip. He scanned the area as he stepped out fully. No one else around. Just the one intruder, dealt with.

The echo of the blast still vibrated in his bones, but now a deeper silence pressed in, thick, absolute. Not a gull screeched, not a car passed. Only the low, persistent buzz of a cell phone vibrating somewhere on the corpse.

Mo stepped forward, his shadow stretching over Tracey's ruined chest. He crouched down slowly, placing the empty shotgun in the crook of his arm like a sleeping dog. The phone was jammed into Tracey's front pant pocket, the screen spiderwebbed but still glowing with a missed call. Mo pried it loose; his gloved fingers were sticky, his breath shallow as he worked.

He wiped the screen on his jacket. The lock screen flickered, then lit up with a new message notification, a voice memo. Mo tapped it open, bringing the phone close to his ear, the shotgun balanced carefully in the crook of his arm.

"Hmm, what do we have here?" Mo's eyes brightened as he examined the phone, stepping over Tracey's lifeless body like it was nothing more than a curb in his path. He spoke to the device with a casual curiosity, almost amused. "What revelation do you have for us today?"

BACK TO THE PRESENT

The cuffs snapped shut around Sloane's wrists, the cold steel biting into his skin. The sound echoed through the room, sharp, final, damning. His shoulders sagged under the crushing weight of his choices, every step heavier than the last. Around him, his fellow officers turned away, some in disgust, others in disbelief, a few with tears brimming in their eyes. The silence closed in, suffocating, heavier than any spoken accusation.

As the officers led him through the bullpen, Sloane caught the eye of his old partner, Russo. Russo shook his head slowly, eyes dark with hurt and betrayal. "You should've come to me, Dane. You should've trusted someone."

Sloane tried to answer, but the words caught in his throat, thick with regret. Outside, the rain intensified, hammering the windows like a thousand accusing fists. The red and blue flashes of the waiting squad car painted the puddles in warning, in judgment, in promises broken.

When the squad car door slammed shut behind him, Dane Sloane stared out at the city, the city he'd tried to outmaneuver, the city that had outplayed him in the end. The last thing he saw was Reyes, standing in the doorway, silent, unmoving, as the rain washed away the last visible trace of the man Sloane used to be.

CHAPTER 30: HE'S GETTING AWAY WITH IT?

The ballroom was packed, the air thick with anticipation and the sharp scent of expensive cologne. Cameras flashed in bursts of white, and applause rolled like thunder through the crowd as Mayor Victor Hensley, the city's golden son and the secret architect of the Ring, stepped onto the stage. His suit was immaculate, his smile practiced and reassuring, a portrait of power, confidence, and curated respectability.

He gripped the podium, scanning the sea of expectant faces. "My friends, tonight I stand before you not just as your councilman, but as a man committed to the future of this city. That's why I'm proud to announce," He paused, letting the applause swell, savoring the moment like a toast raised in his honor. ", that I am running for reelection!"

The crowd erupted, a wall of sound rising around him. But as the cheers began to ebb, Hensley's gaze drifted, drawn like a magnet, to the unmoving shadows at the back of the room. Three figures, silent and still, stood apart from the sea of celebration. Their stances were rigid, their eyes locked on him with a focus that was cold, unblinking... predatory.

Bear Bennett, solid as granite, arms at his sides. Nicole Beemer, arms crossed, chin lifted in open defiance. And Colt Flynn, his eyes dark, hollowed by everything he'd seen and survived.

Hensley's smile faltered, barely, a flicker, and the chill that crept up his neck felt like the edge of a blade. Was that... nerves? The thought repulsed him. No, he was above that. He had control. He was control.

But they knew.

He could see it in the way they stared, not as admirers, not as voters, but as hunters. Hunters who had finally found their prey. The lights overhead now seemed hotter, the room tighter, his suit, suddenly stifling.

He forced his grin wider, held the microphone steady. His voice did not waver. But his heart? It pounded, just a little harder than before.

"I know this city has faced challenges," he continued, voice ringing out through the ballroom, but the words sounded hollow, even to his own ears. In the back, Bear's lips curled into a thin, grim smile. Nicole's eyes narrowed, sharp with purpose, promising justice. Colt was silent but unshakable.

Hensley pressed on, chin high, defiant behind the podium. He had weathered every investigation, dodged every scandal, outlasted every threat. No charges had ever stuck. He had always landed on his feet. But tonight, beneath the swell of applause and the mechanical flicker of press cameras, something shifted. The game had changed.

The truth was no longer buried. It stood at the back of the room, watching. Waiting.

Mo had uncovered encrypted emails, irrefutable threads tying Hensley to the Ring. But no judge dared touch him. Not yet.

He wrapped up his speech to thunderous applause, but the roar felt distant, dulled by something colder. As he stepped away from the podium, he cast one last glance behind him. The three officers hadn't moved. Still as statues. But their stillness was a message: his time at the top was ending. The reckoning he'd always managed to outrun was no longer chasing him.

It was here.

Evil like his never thrived alone. It required complicity. It demanded silence. And it endured because no one dared to challenge the balance. But there must be balance. Between power and justice. Between good and evil. A balance forged not in peace, but in struggle, where every decision costs something, and no one walks away clean.

In the heart of the crowd, surrounded by loyalists, cameras, and sycophants, Victor Hensley stood bathed in their worship, but felt caged. Their cheers echoed hollowly, like laughter at a funeral. For the first time, the city's most powerful man stood exposed. And hunted. With nowhere left to hide.

Looming at the back, Colt shifted. The sling rubbed raw against his shoulder, the dull throb a bitter echo of the price he'd paid. He adjusted his stance, refusing to look away. Hensley stood on the courthouse steps now, basking in the flash of the cameras, the same tired grin plastered across his face. Untouched. Untouchable.

Colt had bled for this. Survived bullets, betrayals, and back-alley beatings. He had crawled through every layer of this city's rot just to stand here, to see the man who orchestrated the Ring, who ruined lives with handshakes and silence, finally brought into the light.

But Hensley didn't flinch.

He smiled.

His suit was still crisp. Colt's blood still clung to his own ribs beneath the jacket.

Rage bubbled in Colt's gut, slow and corrosive. He wondered, not for the first time, if justice was just a myth in this city. A bedtime story for the broken. Because in the real world, men like Hensley walked away clean.

And the rest of them were left behind, collecting scars.

Beemer's fingers twitched at her side, itching to drag Hensley off that stage by the collar. Her badge was the only thing holding her back, a thin, battered shield against the urge to mete out the justice the courts had denied. She could feel every eye in the crowd, some hopeful, most resigned, as the politician spun his story for the cameras. Beemer remembered every victim, every family left in the Ring's wake, the ones who'd trusted her to make things right. The system was supposed to mean something, but tonight it felt like a joke, a cruel performance. She kept her hands steady, but inside she was a storm, her oath to the badge warring with the raw need to see Hensley pay, one way or another.

Bear's eye patch hid the worst of the damage, but his good eye never left Hensley. It burned with the promise of justice, unyielding despite the bruises mottling his jaw and ribs. Each breath came with a stab of pain, but Bear stood tall, arms crossed, a silent sentinel in the sea of onlookers. He'd seen too many men like Hensley, slick, smiling, rotten to the core, walk free while good people bled. The urge to act, to do something reckless and final, gnawed at him. But Bear knew the game wasn't over. Not yet. He'd wait, watch, and when Hensley finally slipped, Bear would be there. He'd learned patience in the sniper hide and on the street, and he'd learned that sometimes justice wasn't a gavel or a verdict, it was a promise kept in the shadows, waiting for the right moment to strike.

Across the room, Silas Shroud melted into the throng, just another face in the restless sea of bodies pressed shoulder to shoulder beneath the lavish chandeliers of the ballroom. The mayor's rally was in full swing, cheers, music, and the drone of speeches echoing off glass towers. Silas's eyes, cold and sharp, tracked every movement from beneath the brim of his cap.

He glared at the three law enforcement officers across the room. His targets: Bear Bennett and Colt Flynn, clustered near the edge of the crowd, their postures tense, eyes scanning for threats they couldn't see. They were quite a sight. Bear still wore an eye patch, and Colt's arm was in a sling. The third female looked like she'd been through the wringer as well. They all looked as though they'd come off a conveyor belt.

How easy this would be, he thought. Although there were three. As he considered it, his gloved hand hovered near the concealed weapon at his side. The plan was simple: wait for the right moment, slip through the crowd, and end them before anyone knew he was there. But as the minutes ticked by, Silas felt the temperature of the crowd change. Too many uniforms, too many restless eyes. Too many variables.

Shroud's gaze flicked to the exits, calculating. The job was complete only if he got out alive. Not tonight, he thought, feeling the weight of unseen eyes and the prickling certainty that the hunters were being hunted. He let his hand fall away from the weapon, blending deeper into the crowd, his face unreadable.

He watched the officers standing stoically at the rear of the room, their watchful gazes missing nothing. They knew danger was close. Silas allowed himself a thin, humorless smile. He'd been paid well, and he always finished a contract. But he wasn't a fool. There would be another night, another chance, when the heat had faded, and the city's guard had dropped.

Before departing, he pondered why they were there. Both targets in the same place. It wasn't as if they were on the mayor's security detail. None wore uniforms. They didn't look like they were on duty. His gaze flicked from them to the podium. He thought: the client, someone with deep pockets and deeper grudges, wanted Flynn and Bennett gone. Hensley's name hadn't come up, but he sensed an overlap. Silas's eyes narrowed unconsciously. "Hensley was the client. Morales was just a middleman."

Silas smiled. He would fulfill his contract, just not tonight. For now, he slipped away, footsteps silent, a shadow among shadows. The hunt was far from over.

EPILOGUE

Alena's journey to healing was a labyrinth of pain, each step forward shadowed by memories she wished she could forget. Every morning, she woke with her heart pounding, sweat slicking her skin as the echoes of nightmares clawed at her mind. Flashbacks struck without warning, sometimes triggered by a scent, a sound, or a stranger's glance, dragging her back into the darkness she'd fought so hard to escape. Anxiety gripped her chest like a vice, making it hard to breathe, and guilt, heavy, suffocating, threatened to pull her under.

She sat on the edge of her bed, hands trembling as she dialed into another counseling session. The therapist's voice was calm, steady, a lifeline in the storm. "You're not alone, Alena. You survived. That's your strength."

Alena swallowed hard. "It doesn't feel like strength," she whispered. "It feels like I'm broken in a thousand pieces."

"Broken things can be mended," the counselor replied gently. "But you have to let yourself heal."

Some days, Alena didn't believe it. But she kept returning, kept talking, kept fighting. The survivor network meetings were raw and real, rooms filled with people who understood her pain without explanation. They listened as she spoke, their eyes shining with empathy, nodding when her voice faltered.

One night, after a particularly brutal flashback, she found herself pacing her apartment, hands clenched into fists. Her phone buzzed, a message from Maya, another survivor.

You're stronger than you think. I'm here if you need to talk.

Alena stared at the words, tears stinging her eyes. Slowly, painstakingly, she began to stitch together the shattered fragments of her life, each small victory-a day without panic, a night with a little more sleep-a testament to her resilience.

Now, as she stood before a small group of new survivors, a fierce determination burned in her eyes. She took a shaky breath and began to speak, her voice trembling but unyielding.

"You will never be the same," she said, her words heavy with truth. "Never. The scars run deep, and you simply have to learn to live with the pain, but the life you knew is gone forever. Fear is a constant companion, haunting every moment, every breath. I still live in terror for my family's safety, and that torment is a relentless shadow that follows me, day after day, night after night."

A young woman in the front row wiped away tears. Alena met her gaze, offering a fragile smile. "But you're not alone. We're in this together. And I promise you-what happened to us will not define us. I will fight so that no one else has to endure what we did."

As the meeting ended, Alena stepped outside, the night air cool against her skin. She glanced up at the city skyline, her resolve hardening. Somewhere out there, Colt Flynn was preparing to return to action.

APPENDIX 1

THE WEAPONS OF RIDE THE DARKNESS

A blow-by-blow rundown of every weapon Colt and his crew used would have killed the momentum of the story. Instead, you'll find a detailed list of their arsenal here, no frills, just the firepower that fueled the action.

Sig Sauer P320 RXP (Chapter 3) This is the latest department issued sidearm that Colt receives when he officially retires. It is a full sized, 9mm handgun with an optic cut and a rail for mounting a light, usually the Streamlight TLR-1, rail mounted tactical weapon light.

Sig Sauer P365 (Chapter 8) Colt usually carries this 9mm XL model as his EDC (Every-Day Carry). He added an Icarus Precision ACE XL EVO grip module and runs a Sig Romeo Zero Red Dot sight.

Glock 19 The thug pulls this standard, no frills, compact 9mm on Colt in Chapter 10 before Colt quickly disarms him and beats him with it.

Beretta M9 The assassin Vic Shaw uses a standard 9mm M9 Beretta with a basic Ultima suppressor when he goes after Colt in Chapter 12.

Martin Acoustic Guitar Colt is forced to use a field expedient weapon in Chapter 12 when Vic Shaw comes after him. This black, Martin DX Johnny Cash dreadnought style, 6 string is all he has close by but doesn't quite hold up to hand-to-hand combat.

Blackjack Another weapon used by Shaw is this short, flexible, weighted baton, typically made of leather or other durable material and containing a heavy core, often lead, designed for striking and incapacitating a person.

Push Dagger – Another one of Colt's EDC items is his Arizona Custom Knives - 2nd Gen Combat PUSH DAGGER, which he keeps on his belt.

Savior Gun/Guitar Case After the battle in Chapter 13, Colt quickly grabs some go-to weapons and hits the road, all in his Savior Guitar-Gun Case. One item is his custom M4/AR15. Chambered in 5.565 NATO, the upper receiver is a YHM with an integrated suppressor (10.5" barrel), complete a Primary Arms lower receiver with a Geissele 2 stage trigger. Colt likes the simplicity of an Aim Point micro T2 red dot reflex sight. Complete with a 1000 lumens Streamlight and a TNVC Advanced Target Pointer/Illuminator/Aiming Light.

Kimber 1911 Also in the case is a Kimber Warrior 1911 SOC3000253 TFS chambered in .45 with a threaded barrel and a Dead Air Mojave 45 Suppressor.

Precision Long Gun Colt didn't get to use his sniper rifle in this book but will hopefully in the next one. He, like Bear, uses an Accuracy International, but prefers the shorter AT-X. Designed for Law Enforcement, this rifle is shorter that the AXSR with a 16.5" barrel chambered in .308. His rifle holds a Vortex Razor HD Gen III 6-36x56 scope.

AI AXSR Bear's rifle of choice, brought out in Chapter 17 at Flanagan's, Bear's Accuracy International is chambered in .308 with a Nightforce ATACR 7-35x56mm F1scope.

Bul Armory TAC Pro In Chapter 20, Colt boasts to Ben about his fancy, highly tuned Bul Armory 2011. An Israeli based manufacturer, the Bul Armory TAC Pro is 9mm based on the 1911 design with double stacked ammo and a capacity of 21 rounds. Colt's pistol sports a Trijicon RMR Type 2 red Dot sight.

Sig Flux Legion Ben's weapon of choice in Chapter 20 uses a SigP320 as its base and then utilizes a Flux Raider chassis to create a unique Pistol-Caliber Carbine (PCC)-style firearm. It has a rapid-deploying stabilizing brace, extra mag capacity and carbine stability. Ben runs an ACRO P-2 Red Dot Reflex sight on his.

Colt 1911 Mo is old school. He therefore carries a no-frills, Government model Colt 1911 Classic, chambered in .45. Iron sights.

Sig Sauer MPX The "wild-eyed thug" in Chapter 20, opens up on Ben with a 9mm fully automatic MPX. This submachine gun is gas powered and extremely compact.

FNX The Shroud carries a .45 Tactical. The FN .45 is a solid tactical pistol and in Chapter 21 The Shroud uses an Obsidian 45 suppressor that he directly threads onto the barrel.

Beretta 9mm - Evan Kane pulls the Berretta APX A1 Compact Tactical FDE on Colt in Chapter 24 from his waistband.

Throwing Knife – Colt uses a Custom Randall Made throwing knife that he pulls from his tactical vest in Chapter 24. Randall Made Knives have a long history of quality knives made in America since the 30s. Colt's are custom made to his own specs and designed specifically for throwing.

Microtech SOCOM Elite Bear uses this pocketknife to free himself and escape certain death in Chapter 25.

Stoeger Coach Gun - Mo' shotgun in Chapter 26, is a sawed-off, double-barreled shotgun. Made by Stoeger, this classic 'Coach Gun' is a side-by-side barreled 12 gauge.

GLOSSARY

Bangs - Flash bangs, a flash grenade designed to temporarily disorient an enemy's senses without causing permanent injury.

BG - Bad Guy.

Blanco - Also known as silver or plata tequila, a clear, unaged tequila that is bottled shortly after distillation.

Code Four - Common police radio communication indicating that a situation is under control and no further assistance is needed.

Code Nine - Another code reiterating that no further assistance is needed.

Comms - Communications devices or radios.

DOPE - Data on Previous Engagement. Refers to the information a shooter gathers and uses to adjust their aim when shooting at different distances, factoring in bullet drop, wind drift, and other conditions. This data is typically organized on a range card, which provides a quick reference for making adjustments.

Fides Amicitia - Latin: "Fides" refers to trust, faith, and good faith, while "Amicitia" signifies friendship.

Flux Legion - A hybrid firearm created by SIG Sauer and Flux Defense, combining a SIG P320 handgun with a Flux Defense Raider X chassis to create a PCC-style platform.

FTO - Field Training Officer. A new police officer recruit is assigned to a Field Training Officer after initial training. They generally undergo three phases of approximately four weeks with three different training officers. They are evaluated daily by each trainer.

Guard - National Guard or Reserves, a unique part-time military force that serves both state and federal governments. It acts as a primary combat reserve for the Army and Air Force and can be deployed for domestic emergencies, overseas combat missions, and to support communities.

Go n-éirí leat - Gaelic for "Good Luck."

IED - Improvised Explosive Device.

Narcan - Naloxone, commonly referred to as Narcan, reverses an opioid overdose. Naloxone works by blocking the effects of opiates on the brain and restoring breathing. It will only work if a person has opiates in their system. Many police officers carry one-use Narcan shots with their gear for overdoses.

Lima Charlie - The phonetic response during a radio check for "Loud and Clear," focusing on the "L" and the "C."

LBV - Load-Bearing Vest.

Overwatch - A tactic where a sniper or sniper team is positioned to observe and provide support to a friendly unit engaged in operations.

PDW - Personal Defense Weapon.

RP - Rally Point. A predesignated spot where the team will meet at a later time.

Reposado - In the context of tequila, refers to a style of tequila that has been aged in oak barrels for a period of two to twelve months.

S.O. - Sheriff's Office.

SIGINT - Signals Intelligence. A type of intelligence gathering that involves intercepting and collecting information from electronic signals.

AUTHOR'S NOTES

Human trafficking is a grave violation of human rights and one of the most pervasive criminal enterprises in the world today. Defined as the recruitment, transportation, transfer, harboring, or receipt of persons by means of threat, force, coercion, abduction, fraud, deception, or abuse of power for the purpose of exploitation, trafficking encompasses a range of abuses, including sexual exploitation, forced labor, domestic servitude, forced criminality, and organ removal. Traffickers prey on vulnerability, using deception and violence to turn people into commodities for profit.

Recent data underscores the alarming magnitude of human trafficking:

- As of 2024, an estimated 49.6 million people are trapped in modern slavery worldwide, including 12 million children.

- Women and girls account for 54% of those exploited in modern slavery, and in some regions, as many as 61% of detected victims are female.

- The International Labour Organization (ILO) estimates that forced commercial sexual exploitation alone generates $173 billion in illegal profits annually, making human trafficking the second most profitable illegal industry in the United States.

- In 2022, the United Nations Office on Drugs and Crime (UNODC) reported a 25% increase in detected trafficking victims globally compared to pre-pandemic levels, with a 31% rise in detected child victims and a 47% surge in forced labor cases.

- In the European Union, 10,793 victims were registered in 2023, a 6.9% increase from the previous year and the highest number recorded since 2008.

Human trafficking manifests in several forms:

- **Sexual Exploitation**: The most widely recognized form, affecting primarily women and girls. In the EU, nearly 44% of trafficking cases are for sexual exploitation. Globally, 60% of girls and 66% of women who are trafficked are exploited for sex.

- **Forced Labor**: Victims, often from developing countries, are coerced into labor-intensive industries such as agriculture, construction, mining, and domestic work. Forced labor now accounts for 35% of trafficking cases in the EU and is rising worldwide.

- **Forced Criminality and Begging**: Victims, including children, are forced to commit crimes or beg, generating illicit income for traffickers.

- **Organ Removal**: A less common but highly lucrative form, where victims are trafficked for the illegal organ trade.

Traffickers use increasingly sophisticated methods, including technology and document fraud, to recruit, transport, and control their victims, making detection and prosecution challenging.

Who Are the Victims?

Trafficking affects people of all ages, genders, and backgrounds, but certain populations are especially vulnerable:

- **Children**: Represent 25–38% of detected victims globally, with rising numbers in both low- and high-income countries. Child sex trafficking has been reported in all 50 U.S. states.

- **Women and Girls**: Make up the majority of victims, particularly for sexual exploitation.

- **Marginalized Groups**: Migrants, refugees, those living in poverty, and individuals lacking legal status or community support are at heightened risk.

- **United States**: Sex trafficking is the most common form, with states like California, Florida, and Texas leading in prosecutions. Over 2,400 federal trafficking cases have been prosecuted since 2000, involving more than 12,000 victims.

- **Europe**: The EU saw a record number of trafficking victims in 2023, with women and girls comprising 63% of cases.

- **Africa**: The region sees high rates of child trafficking, often for forced labor, with most victims trafficked within the continent due to displacement, insecurity, and climate change.

The consequences of human trafficking are devastating and far-reaching:

- **Physical and Psychological Trauma**: Victims suffer from injuries, sexually transmitted infections, chronic diseases, malnutrition, and severe psychological trauma, including PTSD, depression, and anxiety.

- **Social Isolation and Stigma**: Survivors often face discrimination and struggle to reintegrate into society, compounding their trauma.

- **Economic and Public Health Burden**: Trafficking undermines economic stability, perpetuates poverty, spreads diseases, and strains criminal justice and healthcare systems.

- **Community Destabilization**: The presence of trafficking erodes trust, weakens social cohesion, and perpetuates cycles of exploitation and vulnerability.

Human trafficking is a global crisis that exploits millions, generates vast illicit profits, and inflicts profound harm on individuals and societies. Despite increased awareness and policy progress, the problem is growing, fueled by conflict, poverty, inequality, and the adaptability of criminal networks. Addressing this crime requires coordinated international action, robust prevention and protection policies, and unwavering support for survivors.

For more information on how to help stop human trafficking, visit:

- **freedomnetworkusa.org**

A portion of the proceeds from the sale of this book will go to the continuing fight against human trafficking.

FIDES

AMICITIA!

Colt Flynn will return...

ABOUT THE AUTHOR

Craig Michael is a 23-year active police officer. He has been a member of the SWAT team for 19 years and a SWAT Sniper for the last 10 years. He was an FTO and Crime Scene Investigator/CSI. Craig was a commissioned officer in the US Army with 10 years of service in the military. He lives just outside of Pinellas County, Florida and is a proud father of three, grandfather of two and has been married for over 32 years to his wife, Deana. He has an eclectic collection of job experience. He does throw knives for fun but is NOT Colt Flynn.